Bowhunting
Western
Big Game

This 12 1/2 year-old ram completes my 20-year quest to harvest all 28 North American big game species with my recurve. We got all the action on video and it will air on Easton Bowhunting TV on the Outdoor Channel early 2008.

Bowhunting Western Big Game

Fred Eichler

WOODS N' WATER PRESS

© 2008 Woods N' Water Press
P.O. Box 550, Florida, New York 10921

Dedication

To my father, whose enthusiasm for life and the outdoors has always been contagious. I hope to pass these same qualities on to my children. Also to my wife, whose passion for bowhunting equals my own, and to my many other hunting partners and clients, with whom I have shared a great many laughs and memories.

The desire to share our passion for a sport or way of life is a natural progression. I have strived to introduce bowhunting and the joy of just spending quality time outdoors to as many people as possible. It is equally important to protect this way of life so it may be enjoyed by future generations. I am proud to be the author of a book where a portion of the proceeds will be donated to the Save Our Heritage foundation. This non-profit organization was designed to protect and enhance our bowhunting opportunities, now and for future generations. I thank you for your contribution to our great way of life.

Respectfully,
FRED EICHLER

Fred Eichler is to bowhunting what Bo Jackson was to the sporting world. Where Bo was equally adept at carrying a football as he was at hitting a 90 mph fastball, Fred is able to pick up any type of archery equipment and excel at his craft– bowhunting. In a time when traditional bow users resent those who use compound bows and compound bow users look down their noses at those using traditional equipment, Fred ignores the controversy and has fun shooting bows and arrows. Purchasing Fred's book will help anyone who has an interest in trying archery, to get that opportunity. The proceeds from this book will help put archery into schools, city, and county recreation programs, into scouting and 4H programs and the list goes on and on. And, just like Fred, these programs will introduce kids to the joy of shooting arrows and no one will care what bow each child has selected. It's more important that those we recruit into the sport see, through Fred's eyes, the pleasure of using any archery equipment to enjoy the great outdoors.

JAY MCANINCH, PRESIDENT/CEO ARCHERY TRADE ASSOCIATION

Front cover and interior images courtesy–Fred Eichler

Published by: Woods N' Water, Inc.
P.O. Box 550
Florida, NY 10921

Printed in the United States of America
10 9 8 7 6 5 4 3 2 1

ISBN 978-0-9795131-5-2

TABLE OF CONTENTS

ACKNOWLEDGMENTS

This is the part of a book I always skipped reading in the past. After writing my first acknowledgments, I realize that to the author it is really one of the most important parts of the book.

The first time I picked up a bow it just felt good in my hand. After harvesting an unlucky squirrel as a young boy, I was hooked.

I have been fortunate to have met some incredible people in my life, many of whom are partly responsible for me being able to make a living outdoors doing what I love to do. I would be remiss if I did not take the time to mention them here and offer a simple thanks for helping to steer my life in the direction it has gone.

First I want to thank my parents. My father was and still is my hero. He taught me to appreciate and to learn about the natural world, to always pursue my dreams, and to enjoy all aspects of the hunt. Thanks also to my mother for her unwavering love and support of everything I have ever done, and also for taking a little boy to the bookstore to meet Fred Bear, where he signed a copy of his Fred Bear's Field Notes for me.

That book saw more use than any book I have ever had before or since. Fred Bear opened up the world to me through his fine book, and for that and the dreams it inspired, I thank the late Fred Bear. Also, the late Frank Scott, for hiring a green kid to work in Bear Archery's pro shop and museum. His stories were always captivating and entertaining. Jim Widmier of Arrow Dynamics for hiring me as a young man to help manage his archery shop in Fort Collins, Colorado. He has forgotten more than I will ever know about the bow and arrow, and I still hold his friendship in high regard. Blye Chadwick for sharing his time and top-secret hunting spots with me. As a friend and trapping partner, he has no equal. We have spent time taping each other's hunts all over the country and started up an outfitting business together with another friend, Don Ward, who is the next person I owe thanks to. Don was always ready to go hunting anytime, anywhere, and we would figure out how to pay for it later. He also supported and helped with video projects and offered honest advice when asked. Mike Palmer is another friend who has supported me over the years and patiently answered my hundreds of questions. For almost 20 years now, he has shared his knowledge of bowhunting and archery with me. We have shared hunts together all over the country, and I am a better bowhunter and shot for having known him.

Another person I must thank is Jay Dart, who came up with the first interactive video target system. He offered me a job working for Dart International installing the system in archery shops all over the country. It was a great experience, and I met a lot of people who were as passionate about archery and bowhunting as

Client Chris Parrino and a wet gobbler I called in for him in Colorado.

I am. I would also like to thank all the guides with whom I have had the opportunity to work with while guiding clients. Their camaraderie and love of the outdoors have always added to the experience of working outdoors. Jake Kraus has been working with me for almost 15 years. Without his hard work and friendship, I would not have the business or the clients I have today. Cam Keeler is another top-notch guide and friend who is always there for me and our clients.

Also I would like to thank the late Brian Balfany and the late Rob Pedretti. They were both friends and great guides and they are both missed. I also owe a debt to all the editors who have helped me by publishing my articles. They include T. J. Conrad, Dwight Schuh, Don Thomas, Mike Strandlund, Peter Fiduccia, and the Archery Trade Association. I also would like to thank all my clients over the years, as well as all the people who have attended my speaking engagements and seminars or supported the TV show. A big thanks also to Matt Schulte for his suggestions and proofreading, also to Lee Kline for his help and suggestions. In closing, I would also like to thank my wife, Michele, who has helped on this project from beginning to end.

If this has been boring to read, I apologize. Next time, try skipping the acknowledgments.

—Fred Eichler

SCORE CHARTS

Pope & Young Club's score charts for typical American elk, typical mule deer, typical whitetail deer, antelope, bear, and cougar are reproduced in this book with the express written permission of both the Boone and Crockett Club (www.booneandcrockettclub.com) and the Pope & Young Club (www.Pope-Young.org).

INTRODUCTION

Growing up hunting and trapping taught me a lot about the outdoors. Guiding bowhunters has taught me even more. I consider myself fortunate to make a living outdoors. My clients have included hunters from all over the country as well as some of today's best-known bowhunters. The stories and anecdotes in this book are the result of spending an average of ten months a year in the field. Guiding and hunting is not just my hobby, it is what I do for a living.

After almost two decades of guiding hundreds of bowhunters in the West, I have compiled some tips for helping hunters connect on Western game. Although nothing is certain when it comes to hunting wild animals in free-ranging conditions, experience can help you tilt the scales in your favor. The information in this book will help you close the gap on Western game.

This book is primarily focused on helping bowhunters connect on big game. Many of the pictures and stories are of trophy animals. However, I feel it is important to point out that I truly feel that any animal taken with a bow is a trophy.

I chose to make a living outdoors because I have always had a deep passion for everything wild and natural. From the smallest bug to the tallest tree, for me it is all about the sunrises, sunsets, and everything in between. I have always preferred shining stars over city lights anywhere I have ever traveled. Most hunters realize how connected everything in nature is. That is why we make the most passionate conservationists.

I shot this 300+ bull at ten yards. He fell prey to a cow call I used.

1

ELK

Bowhunting elk can be the ultimate adrenaline rush. They are big, majestic, loud animals that can have massive antlers. The elk is arguably the perfect species for bowhunters who want an action-packed adventure. On the flip side, returning home year after year without fresh elk meat or even a close call can be bitterly disappointing.

As an avid elk hunter who has guided more than a hundred clients on hunts for these awesome animals, I have learned that successfully bowhunting elk requires three main things:

1. Getting in range
2. Drawing undetected
3. Proper shot placement

It sounds so easy, just three little things. However, each one has prerequisites. Before breaking down these three main requirements, let's look at some average success rates.

Anybody can bowhunt elk. Go buy a tag, grab your bow, and head out. Obviously, this is as much effort as thousands of bowhunters put into their hunts, since the average archery success rate—including both bulls and cows—in most Western states hovers around 14 percent for both guided and nonguided hunts. Based on these numbers, your average hunter has only a slim chance of ever harvesting an elk.

I point this out because I feel that most people have the misconception that bowhunting elk out West is pretty easy. Heck, just flip on your TV and watch one of the elk shows, and you can see guys calling in and shooting tremendous elk. Some popular DVDs on the market also show one monster bull after another being called into big, open meadows and harvested. Realistically, unless your pocketbook is extremely deep or you have drawn a limited-tag area, your hunt will not be so easy. Statistics from a three-year period show archery success rates for Colorado, Wyoming, Oregon, Washington, Idaho, Montana, and Utah averaging about 12–15 percent. These numbers include bulls and cows and both guided and nonguided hunts on both public and private land. In states such as Nevada, New Mexico, and Arizona, these numbers are slightly higher due to the limited number of tags available.

What statistics don't show are the opportunities lost—for example, close calls, missed shots, and hunters winded, spotted, or busted while drawing their bows. If lost opportunities were included in the statistics, those success rates would be a lot higher.

So what makes the difference between routinely harvesting an elk and falling into the majority of elk hunters who go home empty-handed every year? There are a lot of factors that come into play, some major and some minute, but they all fall under the three main requirements listed above. My goal in this chapter is to help you improve your odds on your next elk hunt.

GETTING IN RANGE

Getting in range sounds pretty obvious. To be able to shoot an elk you must first get in range. Now let's look at how to get that elk within bow range and how not to screw up once he is there. Let's call bow range from point-blank breathing in your face out to 30 yards. This is the critical distance where everything usually pans out or not.

To get within bow range of elk, the most effective and common methods include:

1. Calling: Emulating the sounds of a calf, cow, or bull to lure an elk into range.

2. Still-hunting: Slipping quietly through the woods, hoping to either sneak into range undetected or spot an elk moving toward you and wait or position yourself for a shot.

3. Stand hunting: Waiting in one location for an elk to come into bow range.

CALLING

Let's start with calling. In my opinion, this is the most overrated way to lure an elk into bow range. Any elk that is coming in to a call is ultra-alert. It is looking for another elk, so the odds of getting busted are increased exponentially. Also, since elk use their sense of smell to follow and locate each other, they usually circle downwind of the calls. That said, on those occasions when it does work, when a bull or a cow reacts to your calling and runs into bow range, it is an exciting experience that you will never forget.

Before sharing my suggestions on calling elk, I want to share a story of an elk hunt in Colorado that we captured on video. I was with two friends, and just minutes before we had watched two raghorn bulls sparring in a small clearing about 300 yards away. Now the three of us slipped through the aspens looking for a good spot to set up. I checked the wind, and then moved into an area where I had enough room to shoot. I slowly knelt down by a small aspen tree and started breaking finger-sized branches off a fallen limb. I cow-called softly while my friend Scott cow-called from his position 20 yards behind me.

We had cut the distance in half and quickly set up in a small stand of aspens. We knew the bulls were alone and were counting on them wanting to join up with

This bull came running into range of my two friends and me. Cow calls lured him in to 20 yards.

a few lonely and vocal cows. It wasn't going to be easy—Scott was carrying a video camera and my friend Brian was also with us. Brian was set up to my right and Scott was between and behind us, where he could tape the action if the bulls came in. Scott cow-called again and I broke a few more small branches. We were doing our best to sound like a small group of cows grazing through the aspens, softly calling to one another.

Suddenly, through the trees I spotted the top of a rack as one of the bulls made his way toward us through the white-trunked aspens. He was followed closely by the other bull, which stopped to rake an aspen limb with his antlers. The wind was still in our favor, and the two bulls continued toward us, confident they were about to meet up with some cows, not two bowhunters and a cameraman. As the lead bull closed to within about 30 yards, he stopped and looked around. I was sure one of us would be spotted any second. I tried to make myself small as I hid behind my bow and the small aspen tree. Although I couldn't see them, I was sure Brian and Scott were also trying to stay calm and blend into the brush.

The young bull continued slowly forward, heading directly toward me. If he continued on his current path, he was bound to spot one of us at any moment. I slowly started to draw my recurve. The bull was now only about 20 yards away and instantly spotted the slight movement. He jumped and took a few steps to my left, which turned him broadside to me. Luckily the young bull hesitated while I finished my draw and released. The arrow struck the bull just above the heart, and he ran only 40 yards before he stopped and collapsed in front of us. Our setup had worked perfectly, and Scott captured all the action on video.

Although on tape this whole sequence took less than four minutes, it had taken years of botched setups and hundreds of hours afield to help tip the scales in our favor. What follows is a list of tips and tactics I have used to call in elk while hunting and guiding. Just remember that calling does not work all the time. Wind is by far your toughest obstacle, because most elk will attempt to circle or come in downwind.

NOISE

It's a fact; elk make noise when they walk through the woods. Don't misunderstand me: they can move quietly when they want to, and I've watched bulls that thundered into a setup sneak away without making a sound. But generally, when elk are comfortable, they make a lot of noise: branches snapping, antlers scraping brush and trees, legs and hooves breaking branches or hitting logs and rocks as they walk along. Sometimes they really make a racket. Use that knowledge when you are calling. Noise adds realism. It's tough to get used to because generally when bowhunting silence is your main concern. However, if you are trying to convince a bull or cow to come join you and the only noise is your calling, oftentimes they will hold up out of range. So next time you try calling, add a little noise to your routine. Try breaking a few small twigs or raking a tree with a branch. It may just be enough to cause that elk to rush right in.

STOP CALLING SO MUCH

Overcalling is a common mistake. It's hard not to scream on that bugle tube again or to send a few more cow calls down into the draw. I've learned the hard way that less is best.

Elk have great hearing, and both their calls and yours travel a long way. If an elk is going to come in or respond, usually just a few cow calls (a few being three or four) or a single bugle is all it takes. This can be especially true on public land, where most elk have already heard the latest in new elk calls long before you ever put on your pack.

I once watched a friend of mine on public land spook a bull into the next county by overcalling. From my vantage point above him, I watched as the whole show played out. A bull was heading up over a ridge, and I was trapped on the opposite ridge so I couldn't move without being spotted. The bull was alone and heading into the timber when we both heard my friend's two cow calls float up from the draw between us. I watched as the bull turned completely around and started heading rapidly down the ridge toward my buddy. He couldn't see the bull from his location and cow-called again three more times. The bull continued heading toward him but

This bull was busy raking a tree when I slipped up to 19 yards and saved the tree's life.

slowed down noticeably. The third time he called, the bull bolted back up the slope and into the timber. He had obviously heard too much. I truly believe that had he stopped after the first two calls, the bull would have trotted right down into range. As it was, overcalling blew that elk out of there, and my buddy never even knew the bull was around. I think this scenario happens more than we realize.

The lesson here is to give elk time to respond to your calls. They may be coming in silently from a few hundred yards away, so make sure you give them enough time. I have often been surprised by elk that came in to my calls as much as an hour after I had let out a few pleading cow calls. I try to wait at least 30 to 45 minutes before moving or calling again from the same area. I prefer using a cow call over a bugle and usually use only three to four cow calls at a time.

Diane Kinney is an avid bowhunter who hunts with a recurve. Her story proves how effective calling can be in the right situation.

Diane Kinney from Pennsylvania and her bull that guide Dick Louden called in.

"It was down to the last hour of the last day of my elk hunt, when two bulls stepped out into the meadow across the valley from where we were. I could tell they were bulls, but not how big. I cow-called to get the attention of my guide, Dick Louden. From where he was he couldn't see them. He understood immediately and started calling; the bulls started our way across the meadow into the valley below us and then they disappeared from view into an arroyo. Not knowing where they would come out, I was standing with an arrow nocked, using a pine tree that made the perfect cover for my 'ground blind.' The sound of rolling rocks in the arroyo was the first thing to give away their position. Suddenly there was an elk rack coming up and out of the arroyo, but I realized it was not a legal bull as he passed. I didn't have time to be disappointed when the second set of antlers came into view. This bull was legal and trotting past me at 11 yards. As the realization that the bull was legal flew through my mind, as if on its own, my recurve came up, the string came back, and the arrow was in the air. I heard a CAWACK as the arrow hit hard. The bull's gait changed, he slowed, went about 100 yards, and went down. He never got back up. It was by far the most exciting fifteen minutes of my life and an experience I will never forget."

BUGLING

In my opinion, bugling is probably the most overused calling technique. I bugle only sparingly unless the bulls are really cranked up. More often than not I've seen bulls gather up their cows and run when challenged by another bull. If the bull doesn't run and responds, I try to wait for him to bugle again before calling so I can gauge how worked up he is and mimic everything he does. Occasionally a bull will come screaming in no matter what you do or how often you do it, but generally I try to err on the quiet side. If he wants to fight, don't worry, he will find you.

If you find yourself trying to work one of those stubborn herd bulls that won't come in, try this radical technique. Sneak in as close as you can without spooking the bull or his cows. Then let out your best bugle. If the bull herds up his cows and takes off, you follow. Run up as close as possible without being spotted (terrain obviously plays a role in this method) and then try cow-calling three or four times. Not just a short mew. Stretch it out a bit like a pleading, whining cow. Meeeeeewww. If all goes as planned, the bull will spin around and drop back to pick you up, thinking that he has inadvertently lost one of his cows. In the right situation, this can be a great way to lure in an old bull that usually wouldn't come in to your calls.

Don't forget that most elk coming in to a call will try to circle downwind. So if you're calling by yourself, try to use the terrain to your advantage. Try to force the elk to come in upwind of you, or set up anticipating them to circle downwind. If you practice your calling and hunt during the "prime time" for your location, you may have the most exciting close-range encounter imaginable. When calling, I've had the best luck with two people, one caller and one hunter. I like using two different cow calls to try to simulate more than one elk.

SETTING UP

How you set up when calling will often mean the difference between success and failure. One common mistake is not being set up at all. I have (on more than one occasion) been embarrassed in front of a client when I have gotten busted by a bull charging into range after I had let out just a few calls, hoping to locate a bull. What I have learned is to always be ready and never to call without first being in position to shoot, just in case a bull or cow you don't even know is there charges in. When pair hunting, I like to have the hunter 20 to 60 yards upwind in front of the caller. Exact positioning varies and depends on the elk's position, obstacles, and terrain. In general, if I know the elk's exact position, I like to place the shooter a little farther out between the bull and the caller. If I am calling blind or have no idea if there is an elk within earshot or where it may be located, I prefer to have the shooter within 20 yards upwind of the caller. In certain situations or on heavily pressured bulls, having the shooter downwind of the caller can work great as the bull circles to confirm it's an elk he is hearing.

Using cow elk decoys is a great way to lure in bulls to bow range.

Since most calling for elk is done from the ground, you must use the terrain to your advantage. Most eastern whitetail hunters are used to hunting from tree stands. It is a whole different ballgame when you're on the ground trying to get drawn on an animal that is wired and looking for any movement. My friend and fellow guide Jake Kraus once had one of our clients set up on a bull that was coming in. He told the hunter to kneel by a tree and wait to see if something responded to his calls. Due to cover, Jake was only a few feet away from our client. A bull responded and started coming in. Jake whispered, "Get ready," and to his shock the client stood up! The bull instantly spotted the movement and bolted down the ridge. When Jake asked why the hunter stood up, the reply was, "I always stand up in my tree stand to shoot. I've never shot kneeling down."

If you're going elk hunting, you had best practice shooting your bow leaning, kneeling, sitting on your butt, and standing on one foot. Okay, the last one is an exaggeration, but not by much. Also practice shooting at steep up and down angles. When you do set up to call and stand, kneel, or sit waiting for an elk to come in to your calls, pay attention to your surroundings. I have often kicked myself for setting up in a position that prevented me from shooting when an elk did come in. You want to be concealed, but not so much so that you restrict your ability to turn, draw, and shoot if the shot presents itself. Pay attention to the position of the sun and always set up in the shade or shadows when possible. Whenever possible, I like to set up with my back to a large tree and with a few other large trees directly in front of or off to both sides of me. They can be great vision blockers and can give you the chance to draw quickly without being detected when the bull's eyes are obstructed by them.

Another thing to try to avoid is calling from too open an area. Elk realize something is up real quick when they hear calls and can't see an elk when they know they should. If you must call from an open area with little cover, try using a decoy. Even some of the partial decoys that show just an elk rump or head work great.

Another trick for luring in stubborn elk on pressured land is rattling. I like to use a set of 5 x 5 sheds in areas where I don't have to pack them in too far. Since hunters rarely rattle for elk, it can sometimes fool a bull into range.

Tommy Bender from New York and his water hole bull.

When trying to call elk, I think the best rule of thumb is to let the elk dictate which calls to use and how often to use them. If a bull or bulls are bugling their heads off, hammer back at them. If they are not really vocal, play the same game and tone it down a bit. Don't worry if your calls don't sound perfect. Like people, both bulls and cows have their own unique sounds. Sometimes the worst-sounding bugles and most terribly pitched cow calls I have heard have come from real elk that I would have sworn were hunters.

HUNTING WATER

Another method that can be used with great results is hunting water holes. Find water holes the elk are frequenting by looking for well-used trails with fresh tracks leading into the water. Elk will usually head to water first thing in the evening after being bedded up all day. If the weather is warm, I will sit all day over water. Often, you can catch elk slipping in early in the morning or during the heat of the day for a drink and to cool off. If your area doesn't have water holes or small ponds, you can often find certain spots on creeks or rivers that are favored watering areas.

We often set clients up on water holes in warm weather with great success. A few years ago, I was guiding a fellow from New York named Tommy Bender. Tommy is one of those guys who can tell jokes all day long and never repeat one.

Rob Evans of Wisconsin with his water hole bull and guides Jake Kraus and Cam Keeler.

I wouldn't describe him as a super-patient guy, but he wanted an elk with his bow in a bad way. Problem was that the hunting was slow and the bulls weren't talking much. Since the weather was warm, I suggested he sit at a small water hole I knew about. I could tell the idea of sitting 12 hours didn't really appeal to him, but he said he would give it a try. When I walked in to pick him up that evening, a huge grin met my flashlight beam. He was fired up and talking fast. He explained that a group of elk came in to the small pond just as the sun was setting. He made a perfect shot on the bull and was as proud as he could be with his first archery bull.

Another client, Rob Evans, who is an outdoor writer and avid bowhunter, joined us for an elk hunt. Once again, the conditions were warm and his guide, Cam Keeler, set Rob up in a blind by another water hole.

Rob said: "After just an hour of sitting, I got so warm I stripped down to my skivvies. The heat had me nodding off, but I was jogged into consciousness by the sound of thundering hooves. I dove for my bow and came to full draw as the first cow jumped into the water. Nine more followed, but I didn't see a bull. Then I heard the sound of running hooves again, and a bull ran to the edge of the water shaking his rack. The shot was thirty-four yards, and my arrow blew through the bull's lungs. My first elk made a small circle and crashed dead into the water."

These are two perfect examples of what can happen if you find an active water

This big bull has been doing some serious fighting. He is just dropping his head to get a drink. Now, if he would just turn broadside . . .

hole and wait patiently. Every year, water hole hunting pays off for bowhunters out West. You just may be surprised how easy it can be.

WALLOWS

When scouting or hunting, always look for wallows. They are usually found in swampy areas or sometimes in or near creeks or drainages. Rutting bulls will roll around in these wet depressions and cover themselves in mud and urine. This strong smell helps attract cows and warns other bulls of their presence. Some wallows are used only once, while others are commonly visited and used by more than just one bull.

Wallows are generally easy to spot. The ground and grass around them are usually gouged by the hooves and antlers of rut-crazed bulls. If you don't spot one of these small muddy depressions, you can often follow your nose to them. One of my favorite wallow stories happened while guiding Brian Brochu from New Hampshire. Brian owns an archery shop and is an experienced bowhunter. I had found an active wallow while guiding a client earlier in the season and suggested Brian give it shot. We tried calling a bull in early that morning with no success. So around 10:30 in the morning, we quietly sneaked into the wallow. Brian set up on the ground, and 30 minutes after I left, a beautiful 7 x 7 bull walked in to roll in his wallow. Brian drew back and made a textbook shot on his very first elk hunt.

When you find an active wallow, don't pass on the opportunity to hunt it.

SETTING UP ON WALLOWS

Carefully choose the best location to conceal yourself. Take into consideration where you think the elk are coming from and wind direction. Tree stands, ground blinds, and pop-up blinds are all good choices to use for your ambush.

My favorite setup is the Double Bull pop-up blind because it's tough and can be set up quickly. Blinds are also a plus because they help contain your scent.

I spotted this bull in his bed. After an almost two-hour stalk, I was able to put an arrow into his chest.

A bull will come—it's just a matter of time. Although some people like to call from a stand near water or a wallow, I prefer to remain silent. It is easy to spook a bull that is coming in silently when you rip off a few poorly timed calls.

I don't believe you can ever eliminate human scent, but you can try to reduce and mask it. Clean clothes, rubber boots, and a clean body will help even more. Remember that concealment and scent elimination are the keys when hunting water or wallows because the animals will be close, and more often than not there will be more than one set of eyes and many noses to deal with.

OTHER SETUPS FOR ELK

For other great stand locations, try trails between feeding and bedding areas. Elk, like whitetails, have favorite bedding areas. They also take advantage of agricultural plantings such as clover or alfalfa, where available. Although hunting from the ground near these trails works well, a tree stand gives you a huge advantage with elk. Unlike whitetails, which have learned that danger often lurks in trees, elk are still tree stand illiterate. I usually try to set two stands for different wind directions on one trail. Bear in mind that wind direction in the mountains is tricky business. One general rule of thumb is that wind currents are usually going downhill early in the morning, then switching to blowing uphill by mid- to late morning.

My client Wright Harrell shot this 316 bull from a tree stand. He was set up between the bull's feeding and bedding area.

When hunting active trails from tree stands, don't be disappointed if you don't see anything for a day or two at a time. Elk rotate and often use different trails to get to and from their feeding and bedding areas. Usually they will have multiple main routes they frequently use. Be patient. If you're on a well-used trail, the odds are you will get your opportunity. I also try to place my tree stands on the fringes of bedding and feeding areas. Too much scent at either one can ruin your hunt. Elk don't take much pressure before moving to a new area. Stand-hunting near one of these areas is often the most effective way for a bowhunter to harvest an elk. Unlike a calling situation, the elk aren't as wired, straining to spot any movement or hear a noise. A bowhunter can usually take his or her time and shoot at a relaxed elk as it passes by feeding, on a trail, or coming into or leaving its bedding area. It might lack a little of the excitement of calling in an animal, but it is a great way to put a backstrap on your plate.

ESCAPE ROUTES

This method usually works best on public or private land where there is other hunting pressure. Like most animals, elk have areas they repeatedly use to escape hunting pressure. Finding these areas is sometimes as simple as looking at a topo map of your area and determining where you would go to leave all the people behind. Sometimes it's a matter of trial and error and hunting the same place over and over and noting the differences between where you see elk on opening day and where you find them five days later. Usually these are two totally different locations.

My friend Blye Chadwick and I once lucked into a great escape route on public land when a rifle hunter friend of Blye's told him where the elk usually go to elude pressure from hunters. We decided to try the area on opening day of bow season and watched as at least 60 elk, a few of which were great bulls, all went down the same steep trail heading to another, more remote area. I managed to take a cow out of the group at 5 yards, but more important, I learned an efficient method of setting up and letting the elk come to me. I've had luck hunting escape routes only during the first few days of the season. After that, most of the elk have already moved to their new areas.

When hunting a good escape route, I try to stay on stand all day. Usually these trails lead to more remote areas or areas where the thickest cover or timber can be found.

STILL-HUNTING

Still-hunting can be an extremely effective way to slip undetected into bow range of an elk. Fortunately for the still-hunter, elk are big animals and therefore usually make noise when going through the woods. Most elk guides I know prefer to still-hunt elk if they are with a client who is in reasonable shape who can move slowly and quietly through the woods or run if need be.

Oftentimes elk may be vocal, which makes them easy to locate, but they won't respond to calls. This happens a lot on heavily pressured private or public land. Being mobile often allows you an opportunity to slip up quietly on vocal feeding elk. I have also run into range of elk that hesitated before running, thinking I was another elk approaching. I would only try the run technique on elk that are moving away from you that you can't cut off or catch up to quietly.

Still-hunting requires patience. When I am still-hunting, it usually takes me approximately ten minutes to go 50 yards. That's about one minute for every 6 steps. Slow and steady with no sudden movements is the key. I also stop every few yards to slowly scan the area with my eyes for any movement. I have used this method to harvest both bulls and cows for myself and have also used this method with clients to slip into bow range.

Oftentimes, you will spot elk feeding or walking and can wait for them to come to you or move slowly to cut them off. Full camouflage is the key to utilizing this method effectively. That includes a head net or face paint on your head and hands as well.

One of my favorite times to use this method is when it is raining, snowing, or windy. It really tips the odds in your favor. The key is how slow you can go. I have found that I have never spooked an elk by going too slowly, but I have sent a few hauling by getting impatient and going too fast.

I have successfully still-hunted clients into range of a lot of elk. Unfortunately, since I am usually guiding during elk season, I don't have much time to hunt elk for myself. When I do have a little time, I like to still-hunt if the conditions are right. Since I also love elk meat, I am not picky and usually shoot the first elk I slip into range of. My friends have accused me of having a lucky horseshoe . . . I will spare you the graphic details on where they think it's hidden! I just sometimes seem to be in the right spot at the right time.

My largest bull to date was shot while still-hunting. I was being followed by a cameraman because we were trying to capture an elk hunt on video for Easton Bowhunting on The Outdoor Channel. As luck would have it, we slipped up on three bulls feeding in a secluded meadow. It was early in the season, and the bulls were still hanging out together. There was a small, barely legal 4 x 4 and two 6 x 6 bulls in the meadow. The 4 x 4 was closest and I told the cameraman I would happily shoot him if I could crawl into range. While I was crawling closer, one of the bigger bulls swapped places with the little guy and I had no choice but to harvest the big bull. I am convinced that had I not been wearing a head net and crawling slowly, that bull would have lived another day. Remember that when still-hunting, the slower you go, the better off you are.

Another plus to still-hunting is that you can cover more country. I have often found great stand locations while slipping quietly through elk country. As the old adage goes: "There is more than one way to skin a cat." There are also lots of different theories and methods on how to hunt elk. The ones I have outlined here have all worked for me. However, as all elk hunters know, no method is foolproof when it comes to bowhunting elk.

It's not the size of the elk, it's the size of the experience that matters. Here is my wife Michele with her bull that guide Jake Kraus called in to 10 yards. She used a 48-pound bow, and the bull dropped in sight 70 yards away.

DRAWING UNDETECTED

Okay, you've done it. Your heart's pounding and you're not sure why, but you're also holding your breath. An elk is within bow range—one of the biggest and most impressive game animals in North America. You can already taste those 2-inch-thick steaks. Geez, wait till your buddies see this elk! All you have to do is draw your bow. The shot is a piece of cake. Wait, oh no, what happened? He's gone!

It's happened to me, and as an elk guide I have watched it happen to a lot of clients: getting busted trying to draw.

In my experience, this happens more often than not when you're on the ground in a calling situation. For example, the bull or cow is coming in with every sense alerted. It's straining its highly tuned ears for any sound. Its huge eyes are searching for any movement. As soon as you try to move or draw, wham, you're busted. It's the exception when you get to draw and shoot undetected.

In talking with other experienced elk guides, I have found that they all share similar experiences. I asked longtime friend and elk guide Jake Kraus about his strategy and success rate on calling. He likes to call elk from the first day of the season to the last. He is the best caller I have ever heard and prefers calling to other methods of hunting elk. Here is what Jake had to say:

"When a bull screams within earshot, it makes the hair on the back of your neck stand up! The ability to interact with a wild animal such as an elk is a blast. Not every animal will come flying in on a string. Calling elk is a sport that requires finesse and strategy. It is all about when to call, when to keep quiet, which call to use, and when to use it. If you do it right, you're on your way to a close encounter. Make a mistake and you won't see a thing.

"As with most big game species, female vocalizations are really what the male is listening for during the rut. My twelve years of guiding experience has taught me to use my bugle tube sparingly. I tend to use bugling most frequently as a locator call, and that's it. Using a cow call is by far my favorite and most successful tactic for rutting and nonrutting elk. I'll often emit soft calls every minute or so as I sneak through the woods with a client, probing new areas or experimenting in spots that I know hold elk. A cow call is the best call to use, particularly if you know the herd is sensitive to calling pressure. Once a bull is located, cow calls can either be used to coax the bull to your position or to instill confidence as you move in on him.

"This may sound easy on paper, but remember you are dealing with a wild animal whose senses are put to the test every day. Getting elk to respond to your calls is fairly easy. Getting them in bow range, standing still with a clear shooting lane, and getting a shot without being seen can be very difficult. To further complicate things, by calling you have told the elk that there is something out there. Now the animal is coming in looking for the source of the call. Simply put, the odds are not in your favor. Each year I personally guide anywhere from ten to fifteen archery elk hunters and spend every day of the archery season in the woods. In my experience,

Guide Jake Kraus and Steve Memmott from Hoyt with the bull Jake called in for him.

I would say that only one of every ten encounters ends with success. It's inevitable that you are going to get 'busted,' but if you keep putting yourself in those close encounters, it is going to happen eventually."

When Steve Memmott, the manufacturing manager for Hoyt bows, came out on an elk hunt with us, I sent him with guide Jake Kraus. He loves to call elk, and I knew Steve would be in good hands. The first morning of his hunt, Jake got a bull screaming with his seductive cow calls. The bull was so worked up he jumped two fences to get to them. The bull got nervous when he didn't see his hairy beauty as he closed within range, so he started to turn to leave. Jake turned him broadside with another cow call, and Steve smoked the bull at a little over 30 yards. His first guided elk hunt only lasted about fifteen minutes, but they were all action-filled.

So what can you do to get drawn undetected? Start with camouflage. It doesn't matter if you're on the ground calling, still-hunting, or in a tree stand. This is one of the most important things you can do to help your odds. It's simple. Put on a head net and gloves or face paint on your head and hands, and also wear a good, broken-up camouflage pattern. Don't wear anything noisy. Cotton, fleece, and wool are tough to beat for stealthy materials. I have watched helplessly as elk have bolted from clients when their noisy clothing gave them up.

Quiet down your bow. I once had a client draw his bow as a bull came walking past him heading toward me. I had just bugled again, and the bull was coming in pissed. My client did everything perfectly. He waited until the bull's head was behind a tree and drew. I was about 20 yards away from him on that cold quiet morning and I heard his aluminum arrow screech across his rest. The bull didn't hesitate. He dropped and whirled out of there without ever presenting a shot.

Use moleskin on rests and risers to quiet contact between arrow and rest and to avoid an accidental "clank" on the side of a wooden or metal bow riser. Also, practice quietly removing an arrow from your quiver. These are small things that can save a hunt from being unsuccessful.

Another common mistake is drawing while the elk is not yet at a good shot angle. When possible, wait to draw until the elk is in a position to shoot. I have sat and watched with sympathy as clients who drew too soon had to finally let the bow down, their arms shaking with fatigue when a bull or cow hesitated before coming close enough or stopped when they caught a glimpse of movement. It happens every year, usually more than once. Waiting to draw until the animal is at a good shot angle increases your odds of getting a shot if the animal locks up for some reason. Whenever possible, it is best to wait to draw until the elk's eyes are completely or at least partially obstructed by trees or brush.

The draw itself should be smooth and controlled. If you can't draw your bow slowly straight back to full draw, you need a lighter bow. Every year I see hunters who have to put their bow arm up in the air like they are going to shoot at a star. Then they yank the bow down while jerking back the string. I would rather see hunters shoot a 45-pound bow that they can draw smoothly rather than struggle with a 60-pound bow that is too heavy.

The final key to getting drawn undetected is controlling your nerves. It's easy to come unglued around elk. I have had clients do some crazy things when elk walk into bow range. It doesn't seem to matter if they saunter into a water hole or stroll past on a trail. There is just something about elk that can cause even an experienced hunter to come unstuck. Sometimes it's a situation where a big bull is bugling in your face and ripping up trees . . . well, if that doesn't rattle you then you probably need to quit hunting!

My favorite experience where a hunter "lost it," was in southern Colorado. I was guiding a client on a private ranch and we had a bull pretty worked up, but he wouldn't come down to us. So we slipped up the mountain into some aspens. I set the hunter up in front of me and I let off a bugle. I was just putting the tube down when we could hear this bull come running down the mountain bugling and hitting every tree he could on the way down to us. My client got up and started back down the mountain in a hurry. I jumped up from behind a tree as he came past me and said, "What are you doing? He's coming in." He said, "I know," and kept going. As far as I know, he hasn't been out West elk hunting since. Although this was an extreme example, nerves can cause you to freeze up, or act irrationally.

The best realistic practice I have seen is one of the "interactive" target systems. They can be found at some archery and/or gun retail shops. Watch elk shows on TV

These two bulls are probably 3½ years old.

or rent elk DVDs. They will help you get used to how elk move and react. Shooting 3-D competitions, or just shooting with people watching you, will also help you shoot under pressure. One coach I knew who trained some Olympic shooters would throw firecrackers around to help his students practice under pressure. That may be a little extreme, but you get the idea. Improving your shooting will also increase your odds of bringing home some elk meat.

FIELD-JUDGING ELK

Field-judging a typical rack is much easier than field-judging a nontypical rack. Since the large majority of trophies have typical racks, I have included tips and score sheets for scoring typical animals only. These should be used as a rough guide only. The best way for you to improve your own judging skills is to guess the score on friends' mounts, or anywhere you can observe different mounts, and see how close you are.

Any elk with a bow is a trophy, but for those looking for a record-book bull, here are some tips on what to look for. To make the Pope & Young record book, an American elk must score a minimum of 260 inches after deductions (see scoring sheet). Although there are many measurements that apply to the total score, field judging must usually be done in a few seconds. For a quick snapshot of whether a

Like whitetails and mule deer, elk calves are born spotted.

bull will make the book or not there are a few references that will help.

First check to see if the bull has six points on each side. The majority of bulls that make the record book minimums have six relatively symmetrical points on each side. Next look at the length of the main beam. Tine length can add a lot of score in a hurry, so look for a bull with good tine length. The third and fourth points are usually the longest so a quick check of these is a good indicator. If you can roughly total 55 inches by adding all the tines on one side you probably have a bull that will make the minimum if his main beams aren't real skinny. You are looking for a main beam that is 40 inches or more. Also look at width or inside spread between the main beams at the widest point. If it looks to be 30 inches or wider you probably have a contender.

Each fall, elk grow a complete new set of antlers. This guy is just getting started on his.

I spoke to my good friend Lee Kline about rough judging in the field. Lee has been an Official Pope & Young scorer for over 35 years. Lee said the best way is to count the number of seconds between your breaths after you see the bull. If it is less than one second or you stop breathing completely . . . Shoot . . . it's a good one!

FACTS ABOUT ELK (*Cervus canadensis*)

Elk are often referred to as wapiti, which comes from an Indian word meaning "white rump." Mature cows average 500 pounds, while bulls average 700. Elk calves are spotted at birth and gradually lose their spots after one to three months.

Only the males have antlers, which they shed each year near the end of winter. New antlers are grown every year and can grow at a rate of an inch a day. The rut (breeding season) takes place from mid-September to mid-October. Their average lifespan is 15 years.

EQUIPMENT SUGGESTIONS

Elk are large, big-boned, tough animals. I advise a minimum of 45 pounds bow weight with a minimum arrow weight of 450 grains. Razor-sharp broadheads are always a must. I also suggest staying away from flimsy, thin-bladed broadheads with less than a one-inch cutting diameter.

Elk meat is also hard to beat on the dinner table. I enjoy elk a lot of different ways, but here's one of my favorite recipes, which is great if you're having some friends over for dinner.

ELK ROAST STUFFED WITH GARLIC AND PARSLEY

Serves 6–8

This recipe works best with a boned piece of elk rump.

4- to 5-pound elk rump roast
4 cloves of fresh garlic, chopped
⅔ cup chopped fresh Italian parsley
½ teaspoon salt
½ teaspoon pepper
½ cup olive oil
1 cup red cooking wine
2 cups beef stock
4 to 6 potatoes, peeled and quartered
3 to 4 peeled carrots, cut into 2-inch chunks
2 medium onions, quartered

In a bowl, combine the garlic, parsley, salt, and pepper. With a sharp, thin (½-inch) boning knife, make two or three knife-size holes the length of the roast. Push the parsley mixture into the holes the length of the roast, reserving one tablespoon of mixture. Place the roast in a roasting pan, and rub olive oil and leftover garlic and parsley mixture all over the roast. Let sit overnight in the refrigerator.

Preheat the oven to 375 degrees. Place the carrots, potatoes, and onions around the roast and coat with some of the garlic, parsley, salt, pepper, and olive oil. Add red wine and 1 cup of beef stock. Cover and roast using a meat thermometer to the desired doneness. I suggest medium rare (which is usually about 125 degrees F). Remove the roast and let sit for 30 minutes before carving. Remove the drippings and vegetables and process in a food processor. Add leftover beef stock until it is the proper thickness for gravy. Slice thin and serve.

2
MULE DEER

Of the five huntable species of deer in North America, mule deer, in my opinion, are the most impressive. Besides tipping the scales as one of our largest deer, their antlers can be huge. When you combine these incredible physical characteristics with their keen sense of smell, incredible eyesight, super hearing, and an uncanny ability to avoid humans, it is no wonder that many bowhunters consider a mature mule deer buck to be one of the most difficult species to harvest with a bow.

Before skipping this mule deer chapter in search of easier prey, read on for tips on how to bring home the bacon and an impressive rack from one of these Western giants.

There are many reasons why a trophy mule deer is a difficult animal to hunt with a bow. One is that mule deer are found in huntable numbers in only 16 states. That is a far cry from the 43 states that have seasons for white-tailed deer.

The upside is that—thanks to stricter management in several Western states— the opportunity for a bowhunter to harvest a mature mule deer is as good as ever. Especially for the bowhunter that is willing to go the extra mile . . . literally.

SPOT-AND-STALK

In my opinion, the spot-and-stalk technique is one of the most efficient ways for a patient, slow-moving bowhunter to harvest a mule deer. This method is most successful when the stalk is made on a single animal that is bedded down. In my experience, the two best times of year to stalk bedded mule deer are early in the fall and during the rut. The advantage to early fall is that the heat during the day causes the deer to bed down early and get up late. When the weather is hot (70-plus degrees during the day) deer usually stay in their beds most of the day, getting up only occasionally to reposition, urinate, defecate, or drink.

The rut is another great time to catch a buck bedded. Oftentimes during the rut, an exhausted buck will bed down during the day for a few hours of badly needed R and R. In most Western states, the mule deer rut falls later than the whitetail rut. In southeastern Colorado, for example, the peak of the rut falls in early December. In any case, a buck that is bedded for a long duration, whether due to heat or exhaustion, offers a great opportunity for a bowhunter. Before stalking, you must first spot the animal you're after. The two ways to find a bedded muley are to watch a deer bed down, or to spot a deer that is already bedded. When glassing for mulies in early fall, I rarely see a "mule deer" as such. It is usually a branch that doesn't look right, the flick of an ear, the twitch of a tail, a horizontal line that isn't a fallen tree, or a black spot that turns out to be a nose.

Guide Cam Keeler harvested this 185-inch buck using the spot-and-stalk method.

Using a spotting scope or binocular efficiently takes practice. Most guides I know, myself included, have a particular technique we prefer. We use a systematic grid to cover an area efficiently. Some prefer scanning an area from side to side or from top to bottom. I usually do a quick scan, first glassing anything that looks suspicious. Then I start to comb the area from side to side, bush by bush, tree by tree, and rock by rock. It takes patience and good optics, but once you master the art of glassing effectively you will feel naked without a good pair of binoculars and a spotting scope.

Although I have taken bucks and also guided bowhunters to bucks that I spotted once they were already in their beds, whenever possible I like to watch deer come into their beds in the morning. One reason is that it is easier to spot a deer that is moving. The other is that watching mulies approach their beds gives you a lot of additional information you can use to your advantage. For example, you get to see where the deer came from. Odds are it will be heading back to that area when it gets up in the evening. Another huge bonus is that you can see if the deer you're after is alone or if there are others that are bedding down in close proximity.

In early fall, bucks will oftentimes hang in small bachelor groups. Spotting two to seven bucks together is not uncommon. Unseen deer are one of the top reasons stalks don't pan out. I have closed to within bow range of several bucks that never knew danger was close by until one of their unseen travel partners blew the whole gig. The key to a stalk working out is to know what you're up against. Multiple animals increase the difficulty level exponentially. Oftentimes, due to wind direction, your target, other animals' locations, or the time of day it is best to pass on a stalk instead of blowing the deer out of the area or alerting them to your presence.

It is usually better to wait until things are right and make one good stalk than to try to force things to happen. Wind is always a huge factor in making a successful stalk. Wind currents can be tricky, especially in the mountains or rough country. A very general rule of thumb is that wind currents usually travel downhill in the morning and start turning and moving uphill as the temperature rises about midmorning. In the afternoon they usually switch and start going downhill again.

Before stalking in on a bedded mule deer, study the terrain and choose the best path that will keep you hidden. Also try to choose a landmark near where your target is located. Once you move, everything looks different. I once made what should have been a perfect stalk on a bedded buck, but somewhere along my route I

I harvested this trophy buck using the spot-and-stalk method, and captured the hunt on video.

unfortunately mixed up the rock that the buck was bedded by. When I crept up in range of the wrong rock and the buck wasn't there, I assumed I had been spotted. I quietly headed back across the canyon to my pack and spotting scope and was upset to find that the buck was still bedded in the same spot. I had sneaked up to within approximately 40 yards of the buck while stalking up on the wrong location. I wish I could tell you that this has only happened to me once! A hunting companion can be extremely helpful in situations like this. By working out a series of hand signals, a hunter can often be signaled into range.

Another tip that helps when stalking any bedded animal is to use a rangefinder. I will use a rangefinder to measure the distance between the animal I am stalking and an obvious landmark in front of or behind the animal, depending on my planned direction of approach. The taller the object, the better you will be able to see it. Then, as you are stalking, you can keep track of how far you are from your intended target by checking the range to your landmark.

When stalking, quiet clothing and equipment are a must. Patience is also a good attribute to have. I have watched many bucks slip away unscathed when hunters tried to rush in too quickly.

A few years ago, my guides were impressed when Dwight Schuh (longtime

Guide Jake Kraus, Dwight Schuh and me with Dwight's trophy buck taken on a spot-and-stalk hunt.

editor of *Bowhunter* magazine) and his hunting buddy Larry Jones pulled off a textbook stalk at our camp. They were taping a mule deer show for *Bowhunter Magazine TV*, and Larry was acting as cameraman. On their third day of hunting, the wind really kicked up. They had seen some great bucks from our tree stand but couldn't close the deal. A few days prior, my guide Jake Kraus had glassed several different rut-weary bucks bedding down in a steep draw. The draw was thick with overgrown brush, making it a perfect bedding area. Jake went and grabbed Dwight and Larry from their tree stands and pointed the draw out to them and suggested they try sneaking down along the edge of the draw with hopes of catching a buck in his bed. After a few hours of slipping along and glassing for bucks, Dwight spotted what he thought might be an antler tine in the thick brush. Dwight and Larry took off their shoes and made a great barefoot stalk. On video, Dwight shot what ended up being a record-class buck at 15 yards in his bed.

Six things worked out to make that stalk successful: they had a bedded buck spotted; it was the middle of the day, so the buck was probably going to be down for a while; they had a constant wind in their favor; they took their time; they moved quietly; and Dwight made a great shot. If you're willing to work for it and adapt to the situation, the spot-and-stalk method can help you fill your next mule deer tag.

HUNTING WATER

Oftentimes out West, the biggest mule deer bucks are found in the high desert badlands. Sometimes these areas look more like antelope country than prime mule deer habitat. There is a line in a song I think of when I am hunting or guiding in the high desert plains: "Where the deer and the antelope play." Rest assured that they were not singing about whitetails in that song. Water can be the key to having a successful mule deer hunt. Even if there is a lot of it, all animals have their favorite places to drink. Mule deer are no exception.

I have spent days trying to find out where mule deer I have seen are drinking. Sometimes it is an obvious location, such as an irrigation canal, creek, river, or pond. But sometimes it is like a treasure hunt trying to find the small seep in the rocks or the last puddle in the bottom of a dried-up old river or creekbed. Some of the biggest bucks I have ever seen were drinking out of windmill-driven, metal cattle tanks that are out on the plains, 30 miles from the nearest tree. I have also watched bucks come into alpine lakes 2,000 feet above timberline. The one constant is that all mule deer have to drink.

They also all have favorite places they return to repeatedly. I prefer to scout these areas from a distance whenever possible. A spotting scope is invaluable when glassing water holes from a distance. Although I prefer to hunt over water in hot weather, I have had luck hunting mule deer over water in single-digit weather as well. I have video taped and photographed mule deer breaking ice with their front hooves in favorite areas on ponds and rivers. The point I am making is that by glassing and scouting for fresh sign and tracks, you can open up more options in your

A blind setup near water or an active trail is another great mule deer tactic.

mule deer playbook. River crossings are another water option. By walking rivers or creek edges, you can often find frequently used areas. Usually these are places where the water is shallow or crossing is easy.

If the weather is hot, after finding a frequently used watering location, I like to set up for an all-day sit. Wind direction, concealment, and being comfortable are my biggest concerns. In open country, just getting into position without blowing the deer out of the country can often be tricky. In these situations, I prefer to set up and leave in the dark. When possible, I take advantage of one of the quick pop-up blinds on the market, such as the Double Bull blind. They help contain scent and make it more comfortable to sit all day. Other times, I will try to take advantage of any natural cover, or build a small, low-profile brush blind. When possible, I also like to have multiple setups for different wind directions. A comfortable chair with a back is also helpful when you are going to be sitting all day. Mule deer drink at all times of the day, especially when the weather is hot.

Sometimes when hunting water, you just have to improvise. Last year, while hunting for mule deer in another location with cameraman Michael Leonard, I spotted a nice buck up and moving in the hot midafternoon sun. I guessed he was heading down toward some water and green grass that were located at the bottom of the ridge he was on. I quickly changed the game plan. I wanted to try to get in range of this buck. It was early in the year and there hadn't been a freeze yet, so all the leaves were still on the willows and other trees by the water. We used the thick cover to sneak around and get between the buck and the water. There was a good trail coming down the mountain, and I felt confident the buck would use it. I set up only about 20 yards from the trail, and Mike set up behind me with the camera. I

Hunting over water can be a productive way to harvest your deer. Above, a group of does drink in early September and, below, a young buck breaks the ice to get a drink during a frozen December.

figured the buck would be on us any minute, so we stayed frozen and quiet in our spots just off the trail.

Time dragged on as the mosquitoes busied themselves making us miserable. In my haste, I had left behind my pack with the repellent in it. When you're dumb you gotta be tough, so we both suffered in silence waiting for the buck to show up. After almost two hours, I figured that the buck had either seen us or winded us. I whispered to Mike that we might as well pack it in. As I stood up to leave, I spotted the buck. He had taken another route and was below us by the water. How long he had been there is hard to say. I drew back and shot quickly. I was rewarded with a resounding thump and a beautiful mule deer whose antlers were still wrapped in velvet.

If you're hunting out West and the weather is hot, consider sitting by a water hole all day. If the weather is mild or cold, try to hunt water in the mornings or evenings. It may help you fill your tag on your next bowhunt.

GO HIGH FOR SUCCESS

Although not the most commonly used method for hunting mule deer, tree stands can be highly effective in certain situations. I often use them during the rut on the eastern plains, where mule deer like to funnel through the few strips of trees found along most waterways. I also like to use tree stands when I am hunting near agricultural plantings. Mule deer, like elk, will often travel long distances to feed on alfalfa, clover, wheat, and other crops.

Visibility is one big advantage to being in a tree stand. Plus, if the deer doesn't walk by within range, you can sometimes slip down when conditions are right and make a stalk. Unlike whitetails, which are becoming educated to tree stands, mule deer are still very susceptible to a well-placed stand. The two downsides to tree-stand hunting for mule deer is that mulies are more nomadic than most whitetails. This makes stand placement difficult, and that's why I use them only in certain situations. The other downside is that, out West, it can be a long walk from the truck to where you are hunting.

As I mentioned, we often use tree stands during the mule deer rut when guiding clients for trophy bucks. When guiding Lon Lauber a few years ago, the day before his hunt started, I showed him a tree stand I wanted him to hunt. Lon is an experienced bowhunter and a highly accomplished outdoor writer and photographer. When Lon saw the tree stand I had set up low in a cottonwood tree, he flat-out told me he didn't want to hunt there. It just didn't look good to him. I encouraged him to try it for one full day, and if he didn't like it, I would move him to another stand or we could try stalking a buck. Lon grudgingly agreed to try my spot out for one day. At about noon on the first day, Lon called me to come get him and the largest mule deer buck he had ever taken. Lon explained that it had been slow all morning when he spotted two bucks chasing a doe. The doe led them right by his stand, and Lon nailed a trophy mule deer. Two days later, I put another client, Tom Rothrock from Indiana, in the same stand. Tom also shot a big Pope & Young mule deer.

Before the week was over, three of my four clients harvested Pope & Young bucks, all out of tree stands. The largest that week was a 181-inch monster taken by Todd Wickens, also of Indiana. Todd had seen a few bucks hanging around near some thickets while chasing does, so we set up another stand. Todd's stand was only about 6 feet up, and he nailed the monster buck with a great shot at only 12 yards. The moral to these stories is that while they're not that popular, tree stands can be highly effective for your mule deer hunt if the situation looks right.

SIT FOR A SHOT

Sitting and waiting can be a highly effective way for bowhunters to get into range. One of my largest mule deer with a bow was taken from the base of a cottonwood tree where I had been sitting patiently waiting for hours. I had seen the big buck on multiple occasions and knew he was a true giant. It was a mid-December morning during the peak of the rut when I spotted him following a doe into a dense weed patch. There was some alfalfa planted close by, and I hoped that the doe would lead him into the field that evening. I slipped into the

Lon Lauber harvested this trophy buck with me from a tree stand set up in a large cottonwood tree.

field's edge and set up with cameraman Chris Butt to try to wait the deer out. The

Tom Rothrock of Indiana harvested this trophy mule deer with me from a tree stand. When it was only eight yards away, Tom dropped the string on this Pope & Young buck.

Todd Wickens of Indiana harvested this huge buck with me. He grossed 181 and netted 175 5/8 inches. He was taken from a tree stand at 12 yards.

wind was in our favor, and all we could do was hope my guess would pan out.

Before the sun had even hit the horizon, the doe stood up and started leading the giant buck in my direction. The buck hesitated to rake over a small sapling. While he raked the tree, I could see that this was truly a monster deer. When the buck finished, they slowly made their way toward the field's edge where we were crouched. I tried to maintain my composure as they walked into range. I slowly drew my bow and shot. The arrow passed through the buck's lungs in the blink of an eye. I truly think he didn't have any idea what happened. He took a few staggering steps toward the doe and collapsed. The buck grossed just over 191 inches and netted 186 2/8 inches. This buck, and others I have guided clients on, proves that sitting on the ground, on a log, or on a small stool in high-traffic areas can really pay off, especially in open country where cover for stalking or trees large enough for a tree stand are slim to none.

RATTLING AND CALLING

Mule deer bucks, in my opinion, are not nearly as aggressive as whitetails. So some tactics that work great for whitetails do not get the same response from a mule deer. But that doesn't mean that they don't work at all.

I have guided clients who have successfully rattled up trophy mule deer. I have also had some success rattling in bucks myself. From what I have experienced, mule deer come in much more slowly than whitetails and often need a lot of coaxing. The

My largest mule deer with a bow. He was taken using the sit-and-wait method. For the curious, this monster's gross score was 191, net 186 2/8.

bucks I have rattled in usually had to hear multiple rattling sequences before they would come to investigate. I have had a few young bucks run in, but the old guys seem to really take their time. I have had the best results when trying to call in an animal I have already spotted. The advantage to working an animal you can see is that you can gauge the buck's reaction. If he ignores you, keep making a ruckus.

Once a mule deer buck starts coming in, I stop rattling. I only start up again when the buck stops for longer than 30 seconds or changes direction. In the open country where mule deer are generally found, I really work the antlers hard, frequently crashing the antlers loudly together. This helps the sound carry farther. So always remember to include a pair of rattling antlers in your bag of goodies, but be prepared to rattle more than you ever would for a whitetail.

It is also advantageous to try bleating or using a decoy where practical. Whether I am rattling or not, I always include a doe bleat in my pack. You don't need a special mule deer call. Just take along your whitetail doe bleat tube or one of the tip-over can bleats. I have caused rutting bucks to veer over to investigate when they think a hot doe may be just around the next tree or clump of sagebrush. Mule deer bucks do grunt very similarly to whitetails, and I have heard one snort and wheeze just like a whitetail as well. Although I have tried grunting, I have always had the best luck with a doe bleat or rattling antlers.

DECOYING

Just as with decoying any other animal, I have had mixed results trying to decoy mule deer. The deer may react positively to the decoy and come in to investigate, they may totally ignore it, or they may run out of sight. In states where it is legal, I get a lot more reaction with a 3-D target covered with a tanned mule deer hide than any other type of decoy. No matter what type of decoy you use, it is always best to try it on overcast days. Bright sunny days make almost all decoys shine and look unnatural. I like to use a decoy during the pre-rut or rut. I also prefer using a doe over a buck decoy. I feel that more bucks will come in to a situation where they are looking for love rather than a fight.

Guide Cam Keeler sews a green mule deer hide over a 3-D target to make a realistic-looking decoy.

The biggest drawback in decoying mule deer is the open country they live in. Setting one up without being spotted is the first obstacle. The second is that if mule deer have a long time to look at a motionless decoy, it seems to unnerve them. It is just not natural. For best results, try setting up where the buck won't see the decoy until it is already within 50 to 100 yards. Also, using a doe bleat in conjunction with a decoy will help improve your odds of luring a buck in.

SETTING UP ON A RUB LINE

Mule deer bucks don't make scrapes like whitetails. The biggest scent posts they make are their rubs. You can use this to your advantage if you find the right rub.

Trappers know that if there is only one small bush or tree in a field, every male coyote that passes by will go out of his way to pee on it. Mule deer bucks seem to have the same mentality when it comes to certain rub trees. I call some "one-time" trees, those that have been used only once when a buck was walking by, or it was made early in the season when a buck was working off his velvet. Other rub trees seem to be used as major scent posts, where passing bucks commonly stop to joust and, more important, to leave their scent. I have video taped and watched as multiple trophy bucks have come in over the course of a day to leave their scent on the same rub tree. This is even more applicable in open areas, where there are only so many small trees or bushes for them to leave their marks on. These scent post rubs are usually easy to identify because they get visited frequently, and so the tree or bush gets more ragged-looking every day. These are great spots to hunt, when you can find them. I usually try to set up downwind as far away as I am comfortable shooting, since a lot of bucks will circle or approach these trees from the downwind side.

FIELD-JUDGING MULE DEER

For a typical mule deer to make the Pope & Young minimum, it must score 145 inches after deductions (see score sheet in Appendix A). For rough judging, I look for a typical 4 x 4 or larger, not counting brow tines, since these are usually small if the rack has them at all. Next I look at width. An average mule deer has a 21- or 22-inch gap between ear tips if they were laid out horizontally.

If the buck's inside diameter is as wide as his ears, that's a good start—keep measuring. If I can make 30 inches out of the buck's G-2, G-3, and G-4, it is a good one that should make the minimum. Remember that deep, tall forks add score quickly onto a mule deer rack. This is a quick method I use to figure out if a buck is going to make the minimum score. But there are exceptions, and if the buck's main beam or circumference measurements are weak, he won't make it. If he is symmetrical, he should make it just fine. I look at brow tines as bonus inches that, if present, will just add to the score. The main thing to remember is that if you harvest any mule deer—buck or doe—with a bow, you already have a trophy. A big rack is just icing on the cake.

FACTS ABOUT MULE DEER (Odocoileus hemonius)

Larger than whitetails, blacktails, or Coues deer, mule deer get their name from their large, mule-sized ears. Mature does average 100 to 200 pounds, while mature

An exhausted buck takes a break during the peak of the rut. Notice his swollen neck.

bucks average 200 to 300 pounds. Their average lifespan in the wild is 9 to 12 years. Only the bucks have antlers, which they shed every year near the end of the winter. Mule deer antlers usually branch to form two forks. Fawns are spotted at birth and lose their spots after one to three months. The rut falls in late November to early December. Mule deer are often noted for their peculiar, high-jumping gait: all four hooves leave and hit the ground at the same time.

EQUIPMENT SUGGESTIONS

Mule deer are large, and shots are sometimes in the open. A flat-shooting, fast bow is advantageous. Because of their size, I suggest a minimum bow weight of 45 pounds, with an arrow weight of no less than 400 grains. As always, razor-sharp, sturdy broadheads are a must.

Mule deer meat is excellent. There are a lot of great ways to prepare it, including jerky, roasts, steaks, and stews. The recipe I have included below is just one of many great ways to enjoy your mule deer meat.

PEPPER STEAK MULE DEER STIR FRY

Serves 6–8

You can use any piece of your mule deer for this recipe.

2½ pounds of mule deer meat, sliced across the grain into thin, 2-inch-long strips

6 small cloves of garlic, chopped

½ cup olive oil

2 green bell peppers, cut into strips

1 red bell pepper, cut into strips

8 green onion stalks, sliced into diagonal strips (use the entire onion, even the white and green leafy parts)

8 ounces sliced mushrooms

1 cup sherry

2 cups beef broth

½ cup soy sauce

3 tablespoons cornstarch

In a wok or large fry pan, heat half the olive oil on high heat and sauté half the chopped garlic for half a minute, then add the meat in batches and sauté quickly until medium rare (do not overcook). Remove from pan. Add the rest of the oil, and sauté the rest of the garlic for half a minute, then add the green and red pepper strips, sliced green onion, and sliced mushrooms. Cook for approximately two minutes on high heat. Add sherry and beef broth, and cook for two more minutes on high heat to bring to a boil. In a small bowl, combine soy sauce and cornstarch and stir until fully mixed. Add to boiling vegetable mixture, stirring constantly as it thickens. Add back the cooked meat,stir to cover with mixture and remove from heat. Serve with rice.

3
BLACK BEAR

I shot my first bear with a bow over bait. That was almost 20 years ago now, and I will never forget how quietly that bear moved through the woods. Since then I have harvested 15 more with my bow and guided many clients on successful hunts for these amazing animals.

For those of you who have hunted or encountered a black bear in the wild, you know it is hard to avoid that heart-pounding adrenaline rush—it is like buck fever on steroids. I think it has something to do with the fact that it is both awesome and a little scary seeing an animal that can kill you up close and personal. I should point out that black bears are rarely aggressive and attacks on humans are extremely rare, but so are shark attacks, and who can swim in the ocean without a small thought of sharks creeping in?

The word "bear" conjures up different images for different people. Unfortunately, thanks to a media that often portrays cartoon bears with human characteristics, many people think of Smokey the Bear or Boo-Boo. In contrast, outdoorsmen and hunters usually think of the elusive, powerful, and sometimes dangerous animal that calls most of North America its home. Although black bears have graced magazine covers and have been the subject of many great hair-raising tales, our admiration and fear of them started long ago. Early humans often immortalized bears in cave drawings. Native Americans used their hides, teeth, and claws in ceremonies or as jewelry to be proudly worn and displayed. With all the mystique and legends involving black bears, it's no wonder that the bear has become one of the most sought-after big game trophies.

If you are planning to go after black bears, there are some great tried-and-true methods for bringing home your bear roast and rug.

BAITING

Although controversial, baiting is one of the most commonly used methods for harvesting black bears in the spring and fall. An advantage to hunting bears over bait is that a bowhunter usually has time to evaluate the bear to ensure that only mature boars or mature, dry sows are harvested.

For those hunters planning either a do-it-yourself or a guided bait hunt, don't forget the details. Bears are not stupid. They don't turn off their natural defense systems when coming in to a bait. Be cognizant of the three "S" rules: scent, sound, and not being silhouetted. I advise rubber boots, clean clothes, and a clean body to reduce human odor. Be sure to wear quiet clothing such as cotton, wool, or fleece to cut down on noise. When possible, set your stand up where you have good back cover. If there isn't any, cut some branches and tie in some back cover. Here's another important tip concerning scent: having multiple tree stand or ground blind locations can keep you in the game if the wind switches on you. Many hunters regret shooting the first bear that presents an opportunity, so take your time and try to evaluate the bear.

If you're baiting for yourself, there are several different types of bait that traditionally draw bears in. These include pastries, bread, cookies, popcorn, meat scraps, and carrion. In my experience, beaver carcasses are hard to beat for a favored attractant. Don't overlook hunting cornfields, oak trees with good acorn crops, or other fruit- and nut-bearing trees or bushes. These are all great areas to ambush a bear looking for an easy meal.

This is a huge Pope & Young blond-phase black bear I harvested over bait. This bear netted an impressive 19 8/16.

When hunting a bait site, cornfield, or other bear-frequented areas, don't always rely on the bear feeding on the placed or naturally occurring food source. Oftentimes during the rut, which falls in the spring season, large boars will cruise these popular feeding areas in search of a sow in heat. Sometimes in this situation you need to evaluate the bear quickly and take the shot as soon as possible. I once harvested a trophy blond boar doing exactly that. I was set up downwind of a bait, and the huge blond boar simply cruised by, scent-checking the bait site for sows. I had only seconds to react. My recurve bow drove an arrow into the bear's lungs, and I was able to enjoy some great bear roasts and a beautiful trophy thanks to a quick decision to harvest the bear.

HUNTING WITH HOUNDS

This is another popular method of hunting black bears. The advantage to hound hunting is that it also allows hunters to be selective and increases the odds of only mature bears being harvested. This is usually a very physical and demanding hunt. If you are not in good shape, you will want to train before going on a hound hunt for bears. Most hound hunts are guided hunts. The best advice is to trust your guide. Odds are he knows the country and is used to finding tracks.

Hound hunters use different ways to cut a track. Some guides will "rig" a dog, which means that they secure a dog on a platform in front of, on top of, or behind the vehicle and slowly drive roads in prime bear habitat waiting for the dog to "strike" or sound off (bark) if it smells a bear. Others "cast dogs," which means walking through likely bear terrain in hopes of blind-striking a fresh bear track. Other methods include placing baits out and heading to the bait sites to try to start a track from a bait. I have run bears off water holes in the fall by taking hounds around frequently used ponds or cattle tanks. If you will be running your own dogs, make sure to check the regulations in the state you will be hunting—these vary from state to state. Also be cognizant of where you can and can't go. Most chases cover many miles, so be sure you have plenty of room to roam. I also advise using plainly visible dog collars with all your contact information, as well as tracking collars on all your dogs.

Using dogs to hunt bears in no way guarantees success. Uncooperative bears, weather, and terrain can play large roles in whether or not you will have a successful hunt.

SPOT-AND-STALK

This method is used frequently in the Western United States and Canada, where open terrain makes glassing or spotting the bears more likely. This is also a great way for a bowhunter to test his or her skills. Good binoculars and spotting scopes are extremely important aids to consider when planning a spot-and-stalk hunt. Areas with abundant acorns or berries are prime places to watch when trying to spot bears. During the fall, bears often feed up to 20 hours a day preparing for hibernation. Finding a comfortable spot with good visibility over a large area is a popular way to find a bear to hunt. Once you find a bear, the difficult part is trying to evaluate the terrain between you and the bear and planning the best route to get in range.

Don't buy into the rumor that bears can't see well. In my opinion, being large predators, they just aren't as spooky of movement as prey animals. I believe that

In early fall, bears can often be seen trying to load up on a few more calories before winter. This is a great time to try to stalk one on the ground.

they see at least as well as we do. They also have excellent hearing, and their sniffers are nothing to sneeze at. The good news is that, like most predators, their eyes face forward rather than out to either side, so that, like us, they don't have great peripheral vision. This makes them much easier to stalk than prey animals such as deer and elk, which have much better peripheral vision. Quiet clothing, soft-soled boots, and a face mask or camo paint are all advantageous if you're planning to try to slip up into bow range. When in the open, slow, steady movement will often enable you to ease into bow range. Large, mature bears are even easier to stalk than younger ones, as they have only humans to worry about. Small bears have twice as much on their worry list: people and bigger bears.

In 2006, we guided client Rodney Kennedy from Georgia on his first archery bear hunt. Rodney got some firsthand experience on just how exciting and successful spotting and stalking bears can be. Rodney is a great shot with his bow, and we felt confident we could slip him into range of a nice fall bear. After spotting more than 10 different bears, Rodney made a great stalk with guide Jake on a big black boar. They used the trees for cover and actually sneaked up too close. Jake shot video as Rodney walked around a tree at the same time as the bear. At 10 yards, it didn't take the bear long to realize he better head to a less crowded spot on the mountain. I took Rodney back up to the same area a few days later. Rodney was fully camouflaged, including a head net and gloves and slipped up on a nice bear in an open meadow just before dark. He made a great shot and called me in to help trail the bear. After a short blood trail, Rodney proudly posed for a few pictures with his spot-and-stalk black bear.

Client Rodney Kennedy from Georgia with his spot-and-stalk fall bear.

HUNTING WATER HOLES

Hunting bear over water is another technique I use with great success in many of the dry Western states. In the fall, bears start to grow their winter coats. They are also out feeding up to 20 hours a day to fatten up for hibernation. In Western states, it is not uncommon for temperatures to exceed 80 degrees Fahrenheit in September and early October. This forces bears to search out water, not only to drink but also to soak in to keep from overheating. I have seen the same bear head to water three times in one hot fall day. By looking for tracks around any existing water, it's usually easy to determine the number of bears using the particular water source, as well as their size. A ground blind or tree stand can be helpful tools in harvesting a bear over water. In areas with limited water, this can be an extremely effective way to get into bow range of a bear.

One of the largest bears I have ever taken was shot thanks to a small water hole. It was in the fall, and I was relocating some tree stands for elk hunters who were soon to arrive. I left my truck on a ridge and was hiking down a small dirt road with a tree stand on my back and my bow in my hand. I heard loud splashing off to my left, coming from a small pond not far from the road. I quietly eased the stand down and went to take a look. Because there was so much noise, I assumed a few elk were in the pond cooling off in the heat of the day.

When I reached a spot that overlooked the pond, I was surprised to see a bear rolling around in the water. I wasn't sure how big he was, but I decided to try a quick stalk while he was preoccupied with cooling off. The wind was in my favor,

This bear jumped into this pond to cool off in the fall. Water holes are great places to hunt bears in the Western states.

and I set off optimistically. My plan was to sneak in close and hopefully get a shot as he left the water. The oak brush around the pond was thick, and my only hope of closing the distance quickly and quietly was a large cattle trail through the brush. I quickly made it to the trail, nocked an arrow, and was sneaking down to the pond when I ran right into the bear! He had obviously finished his swim and was still dripping wet when our eyes met. I expected him to whirl and run instantly, but he stood his ground. As I watched the bear's small black eyes staring at me from his huge head scarcely eight yards from my own, I realized how quickly I had transitioned from predator to possible prey.

I have had a lot of experiences with black bears, but this was a unique situation for a number of reasons. First, and most noticeable, at eight yards the bear was huge. He was also only a few steps away, and I was on the ground and alone. Finally, and possibly most troubling, was that he knew I was there and he was not scared in the least. If anything, his body language showed aggressiveness and possibly curiosity, neither of which is a trait you want in a big bear that close. My Palmer recurve suddenly seemed very small in my hands. An aluminum arrow with a sharp broadhead was on my string, but fear and adrenaline caused it to bounce up and down on my rest. The quivering in my arrow soon spread to my legs as the staring match continued. I remember thinking not to show fear because I've heard that animals can sense it. Then I realized it was a little late for that. When the bear cocked his head and shifted his weight forward, I knew I had to react. I drew the string as my left arm brought the bow up to face the bear. My aluminum shaft flashed instantly across the few feet that separated us and drove deep into the bear's chest. As I turned to run I saw the bear crash off through the thick oak brush in the opposite direction. I slumped down into a sitting position and gathered my wits.

I returned later with help, and we found the big bear only a short distance from where I had shot him. My arrow had penetrated through the chest and was lodged in the bear's right hindquarter. Just to illustrate his size, his official Pope & Young score was 20 5/16. To make Pope & Young, a black bear's skull must score 18, which is the length plus the width of the skull. For a grizzly bear to make Pope & Young, a skull must score 19 inches. So this black bear was big enough to score Pope & Young for a grizzly. I think this kind of puts his size in perspective!

Another time I was with cameraman Mike Leonard when we set up on the edge of a small water hole. Bear tracks of all sizes surrounded the small pond, so we knew it was just a matter of time. Just at dusk, a beautiful cinnamon-colored bear came running down the ridge to the water hole. The bear noisily lapped up the cool water. I waited quietly in the brush for the bear to offer me a shot. Finally he moved and gave me the shot I wanted. One arrow later, we were both admiring the beautiful cinnamon bear. It can sometimes happen just that quickly.

Both these bears were harvested in September at water holes. The weather was

My largest black bear netted 20 5/16 inches. I shot him when he was leaving a water hole in southern Colorado. This big bear showed no fear when we were standing face to face.

I shot this beautiful cinnamon-phase black bear as it came down to a small water hole in southern Colorado.

hot, 75 to 85 degrees during both hunts. So the next time you're out West and the weather turns warm, head to a water hole to fill your bear tag.

EQUIPMENT SUGGESTIONS

In most cases, your whitetail setup will work fine on black bears. If you have done everything properly, your shots will be within 25 yards. For bears, I like a minimum of 40 pounds bow weight. I also try to get about 9 grains of arrow weight per pound on my bow. Example: a 60-pound bow multiplied by 9 equals a 540-grain arrow. Put a razor-sharp broadhead in front of your arrow and you will have a great setup.

As with any animal, shot placement is the biggest factor in recovering your game. Pick a spot tight to the crease behind the shoulder and let fly. Due to a bear's long hair and layer of fat, blood trails are often a little more difficult to follow on black bears, especially in the case of a poor hit. Choose your shot wisely. Remember that in the spring and fall, the long hair on the bottom of a bear's chest often misleads hunters into thinking the chest extends lower than it does.

Also, whenever hunting black bear, for safety it is always wise to carry a back-up gun or pepper spray. It's better to have it and not need it than need it and not have it.

All the above tactics are exciting and challenging in their own unique ways. I would recommend one or all to black bear enthusiasts or a newcomer to the exciting world of black bear hunting.

FIELD-JUDGING BLACK BEAR

Bear in mind that most hunters misjudge the size of black bears, thinking that they are larger than they actually are. Here are a few tips that will help you field-judge a large bear quickly:

1. When looking at tracks, bears with 4-inch or wider front pads are usually mature bears.
2. Look for a gap of more than 6 inches between the ears
3. Ears appear very small on the head.
4. A large head with the appearance of a short snout indicates a large bear.
5. Legs appear short and stocky.
6. A rounded chest and belly.

FACTS ABOUT BLACK BEAR (*Ursus americanus*)

The black bear begins life at a whopping half to one pound. After being weaned, the cubs usually travel with the sow, or female bear, for their first year and a half of life before she will force them away. Weights of adult bears can vary greatly based on time of year, sex, and region. On average the boars, or males, are larger than the sows, with an average mature boar weighing between 175 and 350 pounds. A mature sow will average between 100 and 250 pounds. There

This photo shows a mature bear's tracks, both front pad (bottom) and hind foot (top)

are exceptions, and although it's hard to imagine, there are recorded weights of wild black bears over 800 pounds. Black bears are omnivores, feeding on a variety of plant life as well as meat and bugs. Bears are opportunistic feeders and despite having a reputation as scavengers that raid dumps and bird feeders, they are also efficient hunters, commonly hunting and successfully harvesting game, including elk and deer.

Black bears are extremely adaptable and are found in every province in Canada and most Western states, as well as many Eastern states, including Pennsylvania and New York.

Although called black bears, Ursus americanus are often found in different color phases. Colors or shades can vary from coal black to blond.

The potential lifespan for a bear is 21 to 30 years. How long black bears hibernate or even if they hibernate depends on the region where they live and existing food supplies. In some areas, bears may hibernate for up to seven months, while in other regions, such as Florida and New Mexico, they may not hibernate at all if food sources remain available.

Bear meat often gets a bad rap. When handled properly in the field. it can be delicious. However, bear meat does occasionally have trichinosis, so be sure to cook it thoroughly, as you would pork.

Bear scat can often give you clues about what the bears are eating. This sign is full of acorns.

BEAR STEW

Serves 4–6

    3 tablespoons olive oil

    3 pounds of bear meat, cubed (all fat and tallow removed)

    4 small cloves of garlic, chopped

    2 onions, sliced

    1 16-ounce can diced tomatoes

    4 cups beef stock

    6 small potatoes, cubed

    6 medium carrots, sliced

    1 cup frozen peas

    1/2 cup Dale's Seasoning

    Seasoned salt or salt and pepper to taste

In a large saucepot, sauté meat (in batches) in olive oil until lightly browned. Add garlic and onions. Sauté until onions are soft. Add tomatoes and beef stock. Simmer for three hours or until meat is tender. Add

Black bears come in many different colors. One of the most handsome bears I have seen is this cinnamon bear I photographed about two miles from our house in Colorado.

potatoes, carrots, and peas. Add 1/2 cup of Dale's Seasoning and salt and pepper to taste. Cook another hour until potatoes and carrots are fork tender. Serve with cornbread.

4
WESTERN TURKEY:
MERRIAM'S & RIO GRANDE

When most people hear the word "turkey," they think of Thanksgiving or the large Butterball in the grocery store. For hunters, these birds elicit memories of rainbow colored feathers and wild calls echoing from the river bottoms of South Texas to the snow covered mountains of Montana. Although not technically big game animals, turkeys are about as close as they come. Successfully harvesting one with a bow usually takes the same effort and skill that it takes to harvest any big game animal. Please don't think that I buy into the theory that turkeys are incredibly smart. They aren't. They are just scared of everything. When everything eats you from an egg to an adult, I guess you tend to get a little high strung. I do admit agreeing with the many turkey hunters who have said that if turkeys could smell we would hardly ever kill one.

Besides being scared of everything, turkeys have excellent hearing and incredible eyesight. For the bowhunter these characteristics make getting within twenty yards a difficult endeavor. Even though I stated earlier that I don't think turkeys are quite as smart as some people give them credit for being, I have seen them do some pretty interesting things. For example, one of the ranches I guide and hunt on is a working cattle ranch in Nebraska. The rancher's calving season coincides with spring turkey season so that time of year the rancher is extremely busy running around checking calves. Every time I hunt this place, the rancher tells me to hide my truck because the birds will see it and they will act differently. I cannot prove or disprove that turkeys actually recognize new vehicles in the driveway. I can, however, assure you that they can tell the difference between me walking across a pasture and the rancher walking across. I have watched the rancher walk across his pasture without the turkeys even breaking strut less than one hundred yards away. But let me walk across the pasture at the same spot and you should see those birds scatter. Things like that make me wonder if they aren't a little smarter than I think they are.

There are five recognized subspecies of the wild turkey in the United States. The two most common in the Western U.S. are the Rio Grande (*Meleagris gallopavo intermedia*) and the Merriam's (*Meleagris gallopavo merriami*). By the 1920s, wild turkey populations were threatened due to loss of habitat and unregulated

Thanks to successful wildlife management that includes trapping and relocating programs, Western wild turkey, both Merriam's and Rio Grande, are thriving.

market and subsistence hunting. Due to successful wildlife management, relocation programs, and the work of conservation organizations such as the National Wild Turkey Federation, wild turkeys are now found in every state but Alaska, and population numbers are higher than they have ever been.

In the West, Rio Grande and Merriam's turkeys are often found in the same states. However, their habitats vary, causing little range overlap. Merriam's, commonly referred to as mountain turkeys, can be found in foothills and mountains between 3,500 and 10,000 feet above sea level. The Rio Grande, on the other hand, prefers flatlands, rolling hills, and river or creek bottoms at lower elevations.

Colorado is a prime example of a state that supports populations of both subspecies. According to Colorado wildlife biologist Gene Shoonveld, the state has a healthy population of both. The majority of the Rio Grande turkeys are found at lower elevations along the river bottoms in the eastern part of the state, while the Merriam's inhabit the western foothills and mountains.

Although both subspecies are found in many Western states, their physical appearance varies as distinctively as their habitats, making them easy to distinguish. Rio Grande turkeys are dark colored, and the tips of their fans and lower back feathers are tipped with a dark yellow or light brown. Merriam's turkeys have white tips on their fan feathers, as well as white tips on the smaller feathers on the lower back. Occasionally, when ranges do overlap, crossbreeding produces hybrids, which often carry physical traits of both species. Hybrids are rare, since habitat preferences usually act as a natural boundary between the two subspecies.

Although Rio Grande turkeys are scattered throughout the Western states, the majority of their total population resides in Texas. The three states that contain the largest numbers of Merriam's turkeys are Montana, South Dakota, and New Mexico.

A large winter flock of Merriam's turkeys in southern Colorado.

During the winter months, both species form large groups. Usually older gobblers tend to group together while younger gobblers, or jakes (immature males), and hens form large flocks. In many states, snowfall causes Merriam's turkeys to migrate to lower elevations to feed. Rio Grande turkeys usually live out their lives in the same general location where they often supplement their diet with a variety of cultivated crops including corn, wheat, clovers, and grasses.

49

This bird is proudly displaying his feathers for all to see.

In the spring, both species disperse from their large winter flocks into smaller groups, usually ranging from 6 to 20 birds. At this time, hormonal changes triggered by an increase in daylight causes gobblers to start courtship behavior. During the mating season, the long, blood-filled piece of skin located above a gobbler's beak (called the snood) elongates and droops from 4 to 8 inches on mature birds. The bird's wattle, located on his neck, also enlarges and turns bright red. Toms begin to gobble and strut in colorful displays of puffed-up feathers and fanned-out tails. These displays attract hens and allow gobblers to form harems. Once the mating season is in full swing, hens begin to seek out nesting areas.

Between late March and early April, the hens begin to lay their eggs. Eggs are laid one a day until a clutch averaging 9 to 11 eggs is completed. Although the eggs may be laid up to 11 days apart, they will not begin to develop until the hen begins to incubate the nest. On average, the young will hatch 28 to 31 days after incubation begins.

Unfortunately for the turkeys, almost every predator in the West is a threat to them at some time during their lives. Hens and their eggs are especially vulnerable to predation during the incubation period, because the nests are located on the ground. Studies have shown that poult mortality rates for both sub-species range from 70 to 85 percent.

From an egg through adulthood, turkeys provide food for almost every predator out West.

TURKEYS AND THE BOWHUNTER

The most popular way for a bowhunter to harvest one of the Western turkeys is to hunt during the peak of the rut, when mature males, or gobblers, are susceptible to calls that mimic the hen turkey. During the spring, hens will attract males with a series of high-pitched yelps, usually numbering from 4 to 15. Bowhunters who learn to mimic the various hen calls can often lure gobblers into bow range. Decoys, used with or without calling, are great visual attractants that often make the difference between luring a bird into range and going home empty-handed. Decoys alone can act as a confidence builder for wary birds that have grown call-shy.

Scouting for areas that hold good populations of birds is often as easy as going out before the season begins and listening for gobblers announcing their presence. Talking to farmers, other hunters, and game wardens can also help you find areas that hold good populations of turkeys. Be sure to ask about food sources, popular strutting areas, and roost trees (where they spend the night).

When scouting, look for fresh droppings, discarded feathers, and tracks—all are common clues that birds are in the area. All turkeys leave large, three-toed tracks. On mature gobblers, the middle toe will usually measure four inches or more, while a hen's will rarely measure more than three inches. Large piles of droppings can help you locate roost trees. Gobblers leave J-shaped droppings, while hens' droppings are smaller and often with conformation.

Gobblers produce large, often J-shaped droppings, while hen droppings are smaller and oftentimes with no conformation.

Where legal, self-constructed or manufactured blinds can be a huge help in harvesting a turkey. The most difficult thing after luring a gobbler into range is drawing the bow. Blinds conceal movement, which improves the odds of harvesting a sharp-eyed tom. Without a blind, the key elements to successfully reaching full draw are total camouflage and minimal motion.

Whether you choose to utilize a manufactured blind, a self-built blind, or just sit really, really still, there are many different strategies for successfully harvesting one of these big tasty birds. As an outfitter and guide, I have the best success calling birds in during the mating season in the spring. A manufactured blind helps conceal both a hunter and me.

As an avid turkey hunter, I have had success with other, nontraditional methods that don't include using a call. One of the most challenging is trying to stalk within bow range. I have done this only a few times, and usually it works only when the bird you are after is preoccupied with feeding, strutting, or is fighting in terrain that allows you to sneak up undetected. Although this method is only rarely successful, it offers a real challenge for those seeking a new adrenaline rush.

A few years ago, while guiding T.J. Conrads of Traditional Bowhunter magazine, I witnessed a perfect stalk. The hunt started in Colorado, where I had a wall tent set up in a small meadow in the mountains. Soon after our arrival in camp, the temperature dropped and the snow started falling. I suggested pulling up stakes and driving to Nebraska. T. J. agreed, so we packed up our gear and hit the road. The same storm that had been dropping snow in Colorado followed us and was bringing pouring rain to Nebraska. Neither of us quits easily, so we trudged out in the mud and sat in the rain for a few hours hoping a bird would answer one of my calls. We could see some birds feeding on a ridge in the distance, and since nothing was responding to my calls, we decided to sneak around and check things out. We spotted a group of birds just under a ridge, and T.J. wanted to try a stalk. I stayed behind and followed as T.J. circled around in front of the birds and slowly crept up to the top of the ridge. I lay down in the grass about 20 yards behind him as he crept forward. Suddenly, in one quick movement, he drew and shot his longbow. I jumped up to see a bird crashing down in the ravine below us with a wooden arrow planted squarely in his chest. Stalking is not the most efficient way to put your tag on a bird, but if you're up for one of turkey hunting's biggest challenges, give it a whirl.

T.J. Conrads shows off the beautiful turkey he harvested by stalking.

I have also had success ambushing turkeys in high-travel areas. High-travel areas are usually found between roost trees, and where they feed. In the spring, gobblers usually have favored strutting areas as well, which can be identified by multiple tracks and telltale drag marks to the right and left of the tracks, where the strutting bird was dragging his wings on the ground. Favorite roost trees can usually be found in the spring by listening to where the birds (both hens and toms) are calling from before they fly down to feed and mate in the early morning. Underneath favored roosting trees, you will find lots of scat of various ages. Once you figure out where they sleep and where they eat, it is just a matter of figuring out where they usually travel between the two, then setting up a ground blind or just hiding in the brush or field's edge and waiting.

Directly above the huge pile of droppings is a favorite roosting spot. By keeping an eye out for sign like this, you can often find favorite roosting trees.

Although some dyed-in-the-wool turkey hunters cringe at the mention of ambushing turkeys, it can be a fun and successful way to hunt, especially for call-shy birds or before or after the rut, when the males don't respond well to calls. Last spring, I harvested a beautiful Merriam's turkey using this ambush method. The property owner told me that the birds would often leave one of his fields through the southwest corner. After watching the birds cross near a large cottonwood on the field's edge two days in a row, I decided to try to set up on them. I set up a blind about 2:30 in the afternoon and waited. I didn't bring a decoy or any calls, because my hope was to shoot a bird passing by. I had my guide Jake Kraus with me. He was hoping to capture on tape any birds that ambled by.

At 5:30 that evening, I spotted a nice tom and a hen walking in our direction. I woke Jake out of a deep slumber so he could catch the action, or lack thereof, on video. The two birds changed direction three or four times, and each time I thought they weren't going to come by within range. Just as I was about to write them off, the hen turned and walked by at 15 yards. The tom followed and was crossing at close to 20 yards when I drew my 54-pound recurve and sent an arrow through the big gobbler. After a short run, he piled up in the field in front of us. Some may argue that this method lacks the excitement of calling in a strutting tom, but I can honestly say that I was as excited about this bird as any I have taken. To my way of thinking, anytime you can cleanly harvest a turkey with a bow, whether it is a jake with a stubby, barely visible beard or a real rope dragger, you have accomplished something to be proud of.

Another rarely used tactic for turkeys is hunting them at water. Turkeys require water every day. By checking for tracks or by watching birds, you can often find their favorite areas to drink. I have had success in both the spring and fall ambushing birds at water or on the travel routes they use to get to water. When hunting a

Here fall turkeys come in to a water hole to take a drink.

popular water location, I like to sit all day. Birds are used to getting ambushed at water by predators, so they are usually ultra-alert. I suggest full camouflage or a blind if you want to try to shoot a turkey at his favored watering spot.

Many states also offer fall turkey seasons. In many states, you can shoot both toms and hens in the fall, but only toms in the spring. The birds are usually tough to call in the fall, and ambushing them at high-traffic areas or near water is usually your best bet.

When turkey hunting out West, whether it is spring or fall, be sure to bring gear for weather ranging from zero to 90 degrees. The weather can change quickly, and it is not uncommon to encounter heavy snow and freezing temperatures. A few years ago, I had the pleasure of guiding Greg Easton of Easton Archery. The weather had been beautiful and mild until the day Greg showed up. About the same time his plane landed in Colorado Springs, the snow started falling. I took him up into the mountains the next morning, and at 8,000 feet there was about 6 inches of snow on the ground.

The birds were not responding at all, so at 9:30 a.m. I decided we should head to a new area. We drove to my backup spot, which was about 6,800 feet in elevation. The snow was only about 2 inches and melting fast. A lone bird answered my series of hen clucks with a faint gobble. I answered with a few more yelps, and Greg and I sat quietly listening. The next time the bird gobbled, we almost jumped

I harvested this big Merriam's during the fall in Colorado at a water hole.

off our chairs. The bird was close and coming fast. Greg got ready and I turned on my video camera.

The great thing about pop-up blinds is that you can get away with moving without being spotted. You just have to make sure that you only open a window or windows on one side of the blind and not the other, or birds will silhouette you in the open windows.

The bird closed to 15 yards when Greg put one well-placed arrow through the bird's chest. The bird ran about 10 yards and collapsed in the snow. Without winter clothing, this spring hunt would have been miserable.

Although I enjoy both spring and fall turkey hunting, as well as the many different strategies for getting birds in range, I always have the most success in the spring during the peak of the rut and at the tail end of the rut. My standard method

Greg Easton and me with Greg's beautiful bird shot in the snow.

is to try to roost a bird when possible (that is, listen to hear a tom gobble after he flies up into a tree for the night). Then I try to set up about 100 yards from the roosted bird or birds the next morning. I quietly slip in and try to set up where I think the bird will fly down. Usually they like to pitch out into an open area. The key to setting up on a bird you already have located in the tree is not to spook him going in. Take your time and go in quietly. I also prefer to get in while it is still dark to give the bird time to calm down if he does hear something suspicious.

I will often let out two or three soft yelps while the birds are still in the tree, just to encourage the tom to come my way. I also feel that a decoy gives a bowhunter a huge advantage. Often birds will get suspicious if they don't see the hen they are looking for. A decoy is a great visual attractant that often makes the difference in getting that bird in bow range. I like to set up one hen decoy and one jake decoy most of the time. Early in the season, if the birds are still in their large winter flocks, I will set up as many as five decoys—four hens and one jake—to add realism. Late in the season when the birds are split up and most hens are setting nests I will only use one hen decoy. I like to set decoys up close, usually only 12 to 15 yards away. I also like to quarter the decoy toward the blind, since most birds will approach decoys from the front, offering a bowhunter a broadside shot. If a bird doesn't come in early, I will often stay put and call using a series of six to nine

I like to place my decoys close to where I will be set up.

yelps every 20 minutes. During the peak and latter part of the breeding season, gobblers will often cover country looking for any receptive hens. By staying in one spot that you know holds turkeys, you can often call one of these traveling toms in.

There have been volumes of books and probably millions of articles written about turkey hunting and calling. Hens make multiple different sounds, and some hunters enjoy mimicking the purrs, putts, kee-kee, flydown cackle, and so on. But after harvesting more than 30 birds with a bow myself and guiding clients every year, I can honestly say that 90 percent of the birds that are going to respond will come in just fine to a few

This bird came right in to my decoys. When birds strut and fluff out their feathers, be careful when you shoot because they look much larger than they actually are.

57

hen yelps. The other calls can help on occasion, but if you can manage a few hen calls on a slate, diaphragm, or box call you are ready to go.

As with elk, some of the worst-sounding calls I have heard have come from turkeys that I would have sworn were hunters. Overcalling is probably the most common mistake made while turkey hunting. If a gobbler answers your calls and you quit calling, odds are he will come find you. Oftentimes, on heavily pressured public or private land, gobblers will sneak in quietly without making a sound, so be ready.

SHOT PLACEMENT

Turkeys are deceptively smaller than they appear. This is especially true when a gobbler is in full strut, puffed up with feathers flared to impress a hen. The best shot with the largest margin for error is the chest, which is approximately 6 inches in diameter. Broadside shots are optimum, although other angles can be lethal with proper arrow placement.

My guides and I have guided more than 150 bowhunters on successful turkey hunts. We have learned that turkeys are tough birds and can often run or fly a long way, even when mortally wounded. I have actually seen birds that were shot perfectly through the lungs gain flight and lock wings only to expire where they crash

A big mature Merriam's I harvested at nearly 8,000 feet in Colorado. This bird came right into my decoys without me even calling.

A mature Texas Rio Grande turkey I called in. (Note the darker brown tips of the tail feathers.)

down. I have learned through trial and error that there are right and wrong ways to react after you shoot a turkey with an arrow. A lot depends on where your shot strikes.

On turkeys, the two best spots to aim for (to ensure a quick kill) are either the head and neck area or the chest. The chest is where I prefer to shoot, because that leaves the largest margin for error. Even so, the chest and vitals area on a turkey is only the size of two small oranges lying diagonally. The shot angle I prefer is broadside, quartering away or facing directly away from me. On a broadside bird, aim two inches behind and 1 inch low of where the wing goes into the chest. This will put you right in the chest cavity. On a bird quartering away at a 135-degree angle, I come straight up from the leg on my side and shoot at the middle of the bird. This angle will send your arrow through the vitals. On a bird strutting facing away, aim right at the anus to send your arrow through the bird's chest. On a bird walking dead away with tail feathers down, shoot just below the center of the back. What you do

Any turkey taken with a bow is a trophy. Here is a Merriam's jake. Notice the white tips on the tail feathers.

after you shoot will often mean the difference between recovering your bird and not.

First, I advise using a razor-sharp broadhead. I use the same broadhead for turkeys that I use for big game. My goal is a complete pass-through, since that creates the largest wound channel and increases hemorrhaging.

AFTER THE SHOT

The best thing you can do after shooting a turkey is to sit still and wait for your broadhead to do its job. I have made the mistake of immediately chasing a mortally hit bird, only to lose him in thick brush or when he took flight and soared out of sight. If you sit still and quietly, the bird will usually expire within sight or run into the brush where it will soon stop and bleed out. Rushing a bird that is shot through the chest will often cause a bird to fly or run farther into the woods, making it harder to recover.

Unless the bird falls within sight of my position, I prefer to wait 30 minutes before going to recover my bird. Just as you do when trailing big game, look for the arrow first for clues about where the bird was hit. Then look for a blood trail. Turkeys leave blood trails that can usually be easily followed. If you feel that you hit the bird in the guts, or your arrow has stomach or intestinal matter on it or smells bad, give him a good two hours before taking up the trail. Usually he will be dead close by. Gut-hit birds leave little or no blood trail, so you may have to do a grid search. Unspooked, gut-shot birds usually travel less than 100 yards. Check all brush piles or gullies, as birds will usually tuck into a spot where they feel safe and expire there. A bird dog, where legal, can be a big help in recovering a gut-shot bird if you cannot find him.

A head or neck shot will usually cause the bird to flop wildly until it expires. A leg shot that either breaks the leg or cuts major arteries will usually cause the bird to drop where it will bleed out close by. A bird shot low in the leg, whether it breaks the leg or is just a flesh wound, can often be recovered. These birds will usually flop around, allowing a second shot, or limp into the brush where they will quickly lie down. Follow these up after 30 minutes with an arrow ready.

A good rule of thumb is that if the bird is still in range, put another arrow into him. Let your broadhead do the work and treat an arrow-shot turkey just as you would any other big game animal, and you will increase your odds of eating a turkey dinner.

EQUIPMENT SUGGESTIONS

Any broadhead appropriate for big game will work on a turkey. Razor-sharp broadheads are a must. Most turkeys are shot at less than 20 yards, so bow weight is not an issue. Whatever is legal in your state will usually more than suffice.

During turkey season, it's always a good idea to be aware of other hunters in your area. Whenever you're camouflaged and mimicking the call of any game animal, safety should be a primary concern.

Don't pass up an opportunity to bowhunt one of the Western wild turkeys.

These birds offer challenging hunting in beautiful country. So why not supply your own bird for next Thanksgiving?

TURKEY CUTLETS

Allow two strips per serving.

2 turkey breasts, skinned
2 eggs, beaten
2 medium cloves of garlic, minced
1 cup milk
½ cup grated Parmesan cheese
2 tablespoons chopped fresh parsley
Italian bread crumbs
Frying oil

Slice turkey breast pieces into ½-inch strips approximately 2 inches wide.

In a large bowl, combine the eggs, garlic, milk, cheese, and parsley, and beat for 30 seconds with a fork to make an egg wash/marinade.

Place all the breast pieces into the above mixture, cover, and marinate overnight in the refrigerator.

Remove one piece at a time and coat with Italian bread crumbs, fry in oil until golden brown and cooked through. Enjoy!

5
ANTELOPE

Imagine sitting in a small blind in the desert, drops of sweat beading on your forehead and the thick, sweet smell of sage hanging in the air. An isolated water hole lies 20 yards out in front of you, its precious contents steadily evaporating in the heat. Tracks made by delicate hooves pockmark the dirt around the water, and you know it is just a matter of time.

If you have never experienced the thrill of bowhunting for antelope or can't wait to go again, read on for tips on how to plan your archery antelope hunt.

Antelope are truly a Western success story. Hunted almost to extinction in the old days of market hunting, pronghorn antelope are now thriving thanks to progressive game management programs.

The great news for bowhunters is that they are now found in huntable numbers in 16 states. Of these, the four that generally stand out with the highest population numbers are Wyoming, Montana, Colorado, and South Dakota.

After deciding which state you want to hunt, call the game commission and ask for one of the state biologists or a game warden who works in the plains area. Both can be excellent sources of information and will often give you the locations of the best public land to hunt. I have found that game wardens will often give out the names of farmers and ranchers in their area who allow hunting on their property. Once you choose an area to hunt, get a detailed topo map of the region and mark all the natural or manmade water

A lone pronghorn buck silhouetted against a Western sky.

holes. Again, biologists, local wardens, and landowners can be very helpful with this step and save you the extra legwork.

WATER HOLE HUNTING

When choosing a location to set up a blind, my guides and I check all the water holes for fresh tracks and numbers of fresh tracks. Then we rank the different locations on a map according to our findings. We pay special attention to small water holes that are far from any other water sources. These remote places, when found, can be extremely productive. Ranking fresh tracks and numbers of tracks will help you discover which water holes the antelope prefer. Usually it will be where they can check for danger at a distance before coming in to drink.

If the weather is hot and dry, antelope hunting at a popular water hole is the way to go.

Also pay attention to where around the water holes the majority of the tracks are. I have found that most water holes, whether they are manmade (dugout ponds or metal cattle tanks) or natural water sources such as creeks, rivers, or springs, have specific areas where the antelope prefer to drink. Sometimes the reason one area is favored is easy to identify, for example, the terrain or easy access to the water. At other times, it is subtler, for example, firmer ground or better visibility from the antelope's eye level. Whatever the reason, it is always advantageous to learn exactly where on the water source the majority of the antelope drink.

Whenever possible, I prefer to hunt areas with very limited options for water. I also prefer to hunt small dirt tanks or manmade cattle tanks. Smaller water sources are easier to hunt, and blind placement is not so critical. On the flip side, I have hunted large lakes, ponds, and canals where blind placement and scouting the well-used areas is absolutely critical. Make a mistake in these locations, and the

I harvested this antelope when he came to drink at the metal stock tank in the background.

closest look you get of an antelope may be through your binoculars.

Pronghorn hunting over water is a game of patience. Big bucks are just as likely to drink at noon as they are at dawn. So arrive early and be prepared to stay until sunset if you are up to the challenge of a day in the desert heat in hopes of arrowing a big buck coming in for a drink. Weather plays a huge role in whether your hunt over water will be successful or not.

My own patience and determination were put to the test a few years ago while hunting antelope over water. My cameraman, Mike Leonard, was sharing a blind with me. We were attempting to tape an antelope hunt over a water hole for an episode of Easton Bowhunting. I explained to Mike that during a normal dry year, odds were high that we would harvest a buck in a short period of time. Sitting in a small, hot space for almost 15 hours a day is not for the faint of heart. It can take a toll on the most determined hunter. Since I assumed the weather would remain hot and dry, I passed up a few pronghorn bucks during the first few days of the hunt.

A few rain showers made things a lot rougher than I had counted on. After nine straight 15-hour days without another opportunity, Mike and I were starting to show signs of the fatigue and mental torture that only an antelope blind can dish out. Whether it was the heat, dehydration, cramping back muscles, or lack of sleep, it mattered little. We were close to giving up. What started out as a trophy buck hunt quickly turned to a "whatever is legal and comes into range" hunt.

Nine days turned into fifteen, and the fifteenth day of our hunt started out as so many others had. We could see quite a few antelope around us in the distance, but nothing was coming in to drink at our small water hole. It seemed that the many small depressions and gullies in the area were still holding water. The day was slowly dragging on when we heard the sound of running hooves. I grabbed my recurve bow while Mike went for his camera. In an instant, our lonely water hole was teeming with antelope. I was starting to draw my bow on a big doe only about 10 yards away when a large buck walked into my shooting hole. He was about 20 yards away and broadside. My recurve bow jumped in my hand, and my carbon arrow flew right through the buck's chest. The buck bolted from the edge of the pond, dying less than 50 yards from the water's edge. We had spent 15 days—approximately 220 hours—trying to harvest an antelope. I don't advise that type of marathon, but you can bet I was proud of that buck. I'd hunted as hard for him as I had any animal I have ever taken.

Wet weather can shut down water hole hunting in a hurry. If bad weather rolls in, I usually just wait until it dries up before going back out. This is easy for me, since some of my best antelope spots are only a 30-minute drive from my house. For many hunters, however, waiting until it dries out is not an option. In those situations, we either try other strategies detailed later in this chapter, or wait at the water holes anyway, hoping that some antelope will still come in out of habit. I have learned that some antelope get used to drinking at certain locations and will sometimes revisit them even when other water is readily available.

Sometimes pronghorns visit these water holes because the best grass can often

I harvested this 77-inch Pope & Young antelope after waiting 15 full days at a blind near a water hole.

Me and my wife Michele with her first Pope & Young antelope, taken with her recurve bow. The trophy buck was shot when he came in to a cattle tank.

be found near areas that have water, even during the driest years. At other times, it seems they come in just out of habit.

In 2006, my wife Michele had been busy during the first few weeks of antelope season. She was helping our cook feed clients and was also busy helping the guides get hunters out to their blinds. When she finally had a few days to hunt herself, the weather was not cooperating. Another big rain left puddles all over the prairie. Every small depression and road ditch had water in it. I suggested she wait until things dried out, but she had only a few days free and decided to try it. On the fifth day, a large buck literally walked around other water holes to drink at the tank where she was hidden. At 18 yards, she harvested her first Pope & Young buck with a recurve.

Some hunts just seem to be easy and quick. Others can be very difficult and long. A few years ago, I was excited to have Michael Waddell from Realtree Road Trips join us for an archery antelope hunt. Michael had never harvested an antelope with a bow, and he was excited to try hunting them. The evening he arrived, I took Michael and his cameraman out to try a spot-and-stalk hunt. I found a large buck bedded in some tall sage, and Michael and his cameraman made a great stalk on him. They closed to about 70 yards before the buck spotted them and fled the scene.

The weather was hot, so we advised Michael that we thought their best bet would be to wait it out at a water hole. On the evening of the third day, a nice buck meandered slowly toward the water hole where they were hidden. Michael said he was as excited as he has ever been with any animal. The buck came in to drink, and Michael made a textbook shot, dropping the animal within sight of the camera. That night he told me that sitting in that blind for 15 hours a day was one of the toughest hunts he had ever experienced. When it comes to sitting over water, it is usually the patient hunter who scores.

Michael Waddell and his beautiful Pope & Young buck, which he took while hunting with me in southeastern Colorado.

HOT WEATHER GEAR

Since pronghorns are usually hunted in temperatures that can exceed 90 degrees, take lots of fluids with you. A small cooler filled with frozen water bottles will help quench your thirst and keep you hydrated as the day heats up. Stick with loose, comfortable, and quiet clothing. You want to blend in with the black background of the blind, so wear black or camouflaged shirts. Camouflage is also important on any body parts that may be close to the opening of the blind, such as your hands or your face. Keep in mind that

Keep an eye out for snakes and scorpions when antelope hunting.

dangers may include snakes and scorpions, although dehydration and lightning strikes usually pose the biggest risks you will encounter.

In cattle country, antelope blinds must be "cow-proofed." Here a guide strings barbed wire around a blind to protect it from the curious cows (in the background).

SETTING UP ON WATER

Ask permission before building a blind on private land, and check hunting regulations before erecting a blind on public land. Most ranchers and farmers won't mind you setting up blinds, as long as you don't build a permanent structure. The three most common blinds used for pronghorn hunting are partial pit, self-constructed above-ground, and manufactured pop-up blinds. Don't worry if your blind seems to stick out like a sore thumb. Pronghorns adapt quickly and will often ignore obvious objects by water holes, provided they aren't overhunted.

My favorite is the Double Bull pop-up blind. It is lightweight and can be set up in minutes. This is an obvious advantage if you decide to move or set up multiple blinds quickly. Make sure that your blind is as dark as possible inside—any penetrating light makes you easy to spot. After your blind is completed, you should cattle-proof it. Often, where you find pronghorns you will also find livestock that utilize the water holes. A simple and effective way to protect your blind is to drive four T-posts into the ground off the corners of your blind and wrap two strands of barbed wire around them.

SPOT-AND-STALK OR DECOYING

Although bowhunters take more antelope over water than by any other means, torrential rain can ruin such a hunt in a hurry. Fortunately, there are other options. The spot-and-stalk method is tough, since the open prairie that antelope generally inhabit usually offers little cover. This makes it difficult for any predator to sneak up on this sharp-eyed animal. Therefore, full camouflage is a must for trying a stalk. I also advise wearing knee and elbow pads for protection from hot, sun-baked ground and cactus. Broken terrain or pockets of tall sagebrush can be used to your advantage. I have managed to get within range of a few bucks by using deep draws or dry creek beds to slip up undetected.

But getting in range is only half the battle. Drawing your bow undetected is usually one of the most difficult things to do. Practice drawing horizontally and raising your bow slowly. You may have to drop some bow poundage, but it could make all the difference.

For hunters wanting to try another method, there is always decoying. It has been my experience that this is a win-or-lose proposition, with losing being the more common result. Don't misunderstand me: antelope can be and are decoyed in, and it is a rush when one comes charging at you attempting to run off the artificial intruder, often from as far as half a mile away. It is just that the window of opportunity for this method to work is small, and the best results are obtained at the peak of the rut in areas with a high buck-to-doe ratio. So include a decoy in your gear, but be prepared to leave it at camp if your timing is off. Another decoy that can work is an artificial cow or horse. I have had mixed results with these "confidence" decoys, but if you're looking for a project give it a shot.

HUNTING OVER SCRAPES

Another option for speed goats (a common nickname for antelope) is hunting them over scrapes. As the rut approaches, antelope bucks make a series of scrapes. They

Torrential rains flooded the plains, leaving one of my antelope blinds under five feet of water. In rainy weather, try another tactic besides water hole hunting.

also become territorial and constantly patrol their areas to keep out intruders. These scrapes can be seen dotting the prairie and are commonly found in dirt roads or dirt openings out on the prairie. They are similar in size to whitetail scrapes, and pronghorn bucks usually urinate and defecate in them. We have successfully guided clients by placing blinds within bow range of antelope scrapes. So if the sky opens up and your blind gets flooded, try setting up on an antelope scrape. It may save the day.

Here is a story written by one of our clients, Daryl Quidort, about his scrape hunt:

In the predawn darkness, the pickup lurched and bumped through yet another huge puddle, which was flooding the two-track. It had been raining steadily for days. In fact, this part of Colorado had received more than its average annual rainfall in just the past three weeks! There was standing water everywhere. One rancher told us there were full stock tanks on his land that hadn't held water in 20 years.

"And this is the year I picked to come hunt thirsty antelope at water holes," I thought glumly as we followed the muddy wheel ruts in the truck's dim headlights.

Antelope hunting at water holes is normally a hot, dry ordeal. Spending 14 or 15 hours a day, from daylight to dark, in a blind situated near a desert water hole takes fortitude and dedication.

"It's like being in solitary confinement!" one hunter exclaimed. "You can't leave the blind in this open country without spooking all the game within miles. You just have to stay in there and tough it out." Of course, when antelope are coming to the water and the hunter is having action, the day doesn't seem so long.

Sunrise was a bright pink promise on the horizon as we pulled up to the water hole where I planned to spend the day hunting antelope. The headlights revealed the portable blind sitting in 6 inches of water.

"Look at that," Fred's guide muttered in his slow, Western drawl. "All this rain raised the pond." After a short discussion, we decided I should try another spot near some scrapes.

With my binoculars, I studied the scrapes about 25 yards out in front of my blind. I had seen antelope scrapes several times in the past, but never understood them or considered hunting them. Usually found out on open, treeless areas, they look and smell quite a bit like whitetail deer scrapes. I was sure they played an important part in the antelope rut, but I didn't know how. Hopefully an antelope buck would give me a demonstration before the day was over.

About 1:00 p.m., I saw two white specks appear out on the plains. By 1:10 p.m., two antelope bucks were standing 100 yards away, nervously looking my way. They were small bucks, their horns barely as long as their 6-inch ears. After trotting back and forth a couple of times, they both raced

Daryl Quidort and his Pope & Young buck taken by waiting at an antelope scrape.

away at high speed. I wondered if they were afraid of the blind or afraid a larger buck might catch them near the scrapes.

A few hours later, I looked up from my magazine to see a nice antelope buck heading my way. I quickly grabbed my bow and quietly moved the stool out of the way. On my knees, with an arrow nocked and my recurve in ready position, I froze as the buck smoothly picked up speed. He was running right at me. Then, swerving gracefully to his right, the antelope sped past the blind and out of my sight. Without moving a muscle, I waited patiently for him to return—but he didn't. "That's it?" I wondered.

After a time, I slowly opened a small peek hole on a side window. The buck was standing about 60 yards away, shaking his ears and kicking a hind foot under his belly, trying to rid himself of the mosquitoes. Suddenly, he ran toward the scrapes again. This time he sped right past the blind, only about 20 yards away, but going at full speed. Fifty yards out, he stopped, whirled around, and came back. Trotting up to the scrapes, he stopped and sniffed the ground. Then he started pawing the earth with a forefoot.

It would have been interesting just to watch him, to see what his scraping ritual consisted of . . . but I came here to hunt antelope. I shot. The buck's reflexes were to drop and spin away at the sound of the shot. But my arrow got there first.

I know I was fortunate (darn lucky, according to my friends) to get a nice Pope & Young antelope during a rainy-season water hole hunt. Hopefully, if I make this type of bowhunt again, I won't run into such wet circumstances. But if I do, at least now I know what to do when it rains. I'll hunt antelope scrapes.

FENCE CROSSINGS

Fence crossings are the last little gem in my antelope hunting repertoire. These crossings have also saved a few foul-weather hunts for me. In most Western states, antelope will go under a fence—as opposed to over it—90 percent of the time, even when being pursued by predators. This has always seemed odd to me, since antelope are excellent jumpers and can clear a fence easily. I have heard it theorized that this is because fences in the West are a relatively new addition to the landscape and are still few and far between in many states. Most antelope may simply have not adapted to jumping over any obstacles they may encounter. Sadly enough, in the future, as fences become more frequently encountered obstacles, antelope will probably become accustomed to jumping over them.

Since they prefer going under rather than over fences, there are always certain places along fence lines where you will find well-worn trails. Antelope often walk quite a ways to use these favored crossing spots where, due to the terrain or a broken strand in the fence, it is easier to go under. If you find a good one, don't pass up an opportunity to harvest your buck there. If the farmer or rancher doesn't mind, you can make your own fence crossing. Just use a few twists of bailing wire or twine to raise the bottom wire by tying it to the one above it. It may not be good to hunt until the following year, but you can bet that the antelope will find and use it.

When approaching a fence crossing, antelope usually stop for a few seconds before going under. That is a perfect opportunity for a bowhunter to take a standing broadside shot. Blinds should be set up near the fence, as far away as you can comfortably shoot. For example, if you're comfortable shooting out to 25 yards, set up the blind 25 yards from the crossing.

Years ago, I shot a beautiful young buck at a fence crossing. I found an active fence crossing and set up a blind about 20 yards from the trail. The weather had been pretty bad, so the water hole hunting was slow. I climbed into the blind early the next morning. After only a couple of hours, a group of young bucks came walking across the pasture heading toward my ambush point. When the lead buck reached the fence, he stopped to look things over. My arrow

A trophy antelope gives me the stare-down.

passed through his chest, and a short sprint later he fell within sight of my blind.

I feel that fence crossings are not nearly as productive as water holes in hot, dry weather, but they do provide another enjoyable way to hunt the prairie speedsters.

When hunting antelope, remember that they have incredible eyesight that they rely on to a fault. Although they have great hearing and olfactory senses, in most cases they just don't seem to believe that danger is there unless they can see it. Their eyes are their main means of defense. If you can fool their eyes, you are on your way to harvesting what is, in my opinion, the most desirable Western big game animal.

FIELD-JUDGING ANTELOPE

For bowhunters interested in trophy antelope, it is important to be able to accurately field-judge a buck. To make the Pope & Young record book, antelope must have a minimum score of 67 inches. Antelope can be difficult to judge, because they have few measurements and no width measurement. This means the few measurements that they do get have a large bearing on your final score. Instead of trying to break down the intricacies of measuring, I will detail how to quickly judge whether you are looking at a trophy animal.

On average, an antelope's ear is 6 inches from tip to base. If the antelope has horns that are 13 inches or longer, you may have a contender. So the first thing I do is quickly look to see if the antelope's horn is a little longer than twice the length of his ears. Don't forget that an antelope's main horn is often curved at the tip, so this will add to the length. I have seen some with 4 inches of curl-over, so keep that in mind.

Next, look at the prong, or cutter, as it is often called. Again, use the ear for a reference. If there is more than half an ear showing, or 3 inches, keep looking.

My largest antelope, harvested in Colorado, netted an impressive 79 inches.

Circumference is the next thing to look at. Antelope horns are oblong rather than round, making them wide at the sides and thin in the front and back, so to rough-judge mass you want to try to get a side view if possible. Instead of looking at and trying to guess all four circumference measurements, I look at the widest or thickest part of the horn, which is between the base and the prong. If it looks like it is 2 1/2 inches wide, it probably has close to a 6- to 7-inch base. Unless it gets really skinny really quickly at the top, it should make the minimum.

Other things I look for are prongs that start above the ears, or really heavy mass that carries the length of the horn. Of course this is a quick, rough way to estimate if what you're looking at will make the record book. I think if you shoot any antelope with a bow, you already have a trophy. Large horns are just icing on the cake.

FACTS ABOUT ANTELOPE (Antilocapra americana)

Antelope, or pronghorns as they are commonly called due to their two-pronged horns, are as unique as the open prairies they call home. Evolution helped these animals adapt to the prairies they live in by developing many different distinguishing characteristics. One of the most notable is their headgear, which they shed every year in November or December. Although called a horn, it really isn't a true horn, since true horns—like those of bighorn sheep or Rocky Mountain goats—grow continually throughout the animal's lifetime. Antelope bucks have a bone core that is covered by a black outer sheath made of keratin. Keratin is a tough, insoluble protein substance that is the chief constituent of hair, nails, horns, and hooves. Oddly enough, about 40 percent of mature doe antelope also grow horns, but unlike the buck horns, which average 13 to 15 inches in height, does' horns rarely grow more than 4 inches long. When antelope shed their horns in November or December, a new sheath, wrapped in hair, is already beginning to grow. Unlike antlers, which grow from the base, antelope horns grow their sheaths both up and down, starting from the tip of the core.

These three antelope does are enjoying a drink during the heat of the day.

Although they appear huge on the open prairies they inhabit, antelope bucks average only 120 pounds, while the smaller does average 105 pounds. They are equipped with lightning speed, which helps them outdistance their predators, since hiding in the open isn't really an option. The fastest land animals in North America, antelope can achieve speeds of up to 60 miles per hour for short bursts, and they can maintain speeds of 30 to 40 miles per hour for long distances over uneven terrain.

Pronghorns also come equipped with spongy, hollow hair that provides layering warmth in the subzero temperatures and blistering winds they face in the winter. In the summertime, temperatures on the Western plains and deserts often exceed 100 degrees. When the weather turns warm, antelope shed their spongy coats, which helps to cool them down. Additionally, they can cause their remaining hairs to stand upright, which helps air circulate close to the skin, keeping them from overheating.

Their protruding, side-mounted eyes allow them close to a 270-degree field of view, which makes slipping up on one undetected very, very difficult.

Antelope fawns are born with muted brown and white coats that become more pronounced and obvious as they mature.

As you can see, antelope are uniquely suited for only one type of habitat. If we ever lose the large tracts of open prairies and grasslands, I fear we will lose or endanger one of the most impressive animals that shares the West with us.

Even if you never plan to bowhunt for antelope, next time you're out West, take a drive out to see one. A large herd running in unison across a seemingly endless prairie is truly a sight to behold.

EQUIPMENT SUGGESTIONS

Antelope are small animals, so arrow penetration is rarely an issue. I advise a minimum of 40 pounds of bow weight, with 9 grains of arrow weight per pound of your bow. For example, a 40-pound bow would require a 360-grain arrow. And as always, a razor-sharp broadhead is a must. Choose a quiet bow that is as short as possible, whether you are shooting a traditional bow or a compound. Shorter bows are easier to maneuver inside a blind.

GRILLED ANTELOPE BACKSTRAP

Allow 6–8 ounces per serving. This marinade works great with elk and deer also.

1 cup soy sauce
½ cup olive oil
½ cup A1 Steak Sauce
4 large cloves of garlic, chopped
½ cup chopped onion
1 tablespoon Jane's Krazy Mixed-up Salt or similar seasoned salt with garlic
2 tablespoons Grill Mates Montreal Steak Seasoning

In a non-metallic container, combine all the ingredients. Add whole antelope backstraps. Make sure the marinade covers the meat. Marinate backstraps overnight. Discard leftover marinade.

Grill to desired doneness. Slice across the grain into ½-inch-thick slices. Game should never be overcooked, as it has less fat than beef. Medium rare to medium is our preference.

Whitetail bucks like this west Kansas brute follow water drainages west into the Rocky Mountain states.

This bull came running in to a series of cow calls.

It's nice to glass a hillside without seeing other hunters.

I managed to stalk up on this trophy bull while he was feeding in a small meadow.

Me and client Brian Bochu from New Hampshire with his first bull elk. He harvested this beautiful 7 x 7 over a wallow where I had set him up.

A beautiful early season mule deer in velvet. I took this buck during a hot fall day while he was making his way down the ridge to some water.

A local rancher called to say he found this tom's tracks on his ranch.

Outdoor writer Dave Holt and his beautiful Pope & Young 4 x 4 taken from the ground.

A good clean shot is your goal!

This is a huge Pope & Young blonde-phase black bear I harvested over bait. This bear netted an impressive 19 $\frac{8}{16}$.

This record-book boar followed a hot sow into a bait site where I was waiting.

I shot this antelope as he was coming in for a drink in the middle of the day.

My wife Michele with a trophy mule deer she called in with a doe bleat. He came in from two hundred yards and was shot at 11 yards.

I harvested this Pope & Young mule deer from a tree stand.

One of my clients with a nice 6 x 6 bull that was called into range by one of my guides.

Elk are big animals that can have huge antlers. They also taste great. What's not to like?

6
WHITE-TAILED DEER

Many of the Western states have always been known for their trophy mule deer. Now many of those same states are rapidly earning a reputation for being trophy whitetail destinations as well. Colorado, Wyoming, Montana, and the Dakotas stand out as Western states that are now home to both trophy mule deer and whitetails.

The West is still predominantly mule deer country, but whitetails have infiltrated into the West via the lower elevation-river drainages, creek bottoms, and farmland found mostly on the eastern sides of these states.

In some areas, both whitetails and mule deer coexist in the same habitat. This occasionally causes crossbreeding, which can result in deer with certain traits of both whitetails and mule deer.

My wife Michele shot this beautiful whitetail buck in Montana.

White-tailed deer are found in huntable numbers in 43 states. The most abundant big game animals in North America, whitetails are rapidly gaining in popularity in the West.

Many states don't offer different tags for the two different species. For

Be careful when setting up tree stands in large cottonwood trees out West. The bark is thick and not stable.

example, in Colorado your deer tag is good for either a whitetail or a mule deer. This is great for your average bowhunter, who would happily shoot either species if they wandered by within range.

A few years ago, my wife Michele—an avid bowhunter and CEO of Muzzy Products—shot a trophy whitetail in Montana's Milk River basin. She took the buck from a tree stand while he was feeding in a farm field.

Most Western whitetails are found at lower elevations near water sources with agricultural plantings close by. There are exceptions, however, and I have seen whitetails as high as 8,000 feet above sea level and out in the middle of large sage prairies 40 miles from the closest farmland or water drainage.

GLASSING

When hunting Western whitetails, I employ many of the same methods that I use in the East and Midwest—with one exception—high-quality optics play a big role in scouting the more open Western states. This is where visibility can extend over many miles of relatively treeless country. For me, a spotting scope and good binoculars are as important as my bow. The advantage of glassing a lot of country is that whitetails are not as abundant out West and are usually found in concentrated numbers where they have food, water, and cover. By glassing and observing their favored trails and bedding and feeding areas, you can figure out where to hunt without blowing deer out of an area. Another plus is you can often pattern one specific buck.

Early in the fall, white-tailed deer can be ambushed along trails between their feeding and bedding areas. This is usually the easiest time of year to pattern specific bucks. Well-constructed ground blinds or pop-up blinds that have been brushed in can work well along trails or in areas where there are no trees to hang a tree stand. Whenever possible, I prefer to hunt whitetails from a tree stand. The only problem with tree stands out West is that the most common trees along water drainages are cottonwoods. These trees are usually large-trunked and rarely straight, so finding a good tree is like hitting the lottery. Be prepared to have extra chains or straps to get stands into large or tilted trees. Check with the manufacturer of the stand you use so you don't void any warranties or put yourself in a dangerous situation.

The other problem with cottonwood trees is their thick bark, which usually won't allow steps to get a good grip on the actual wood of the tree. This can be solved by using an ax to clear the deep bark where you want to place steps, or by using some of the strap-on ladders available.

The next obstacle you will often face is cover. Cottonwoods are large-leafed trees that may provide a little cover in early fall, but when the leaves drop they often leave a bowhunter sticking out like a sore thumb. I often tie up brush using baling wire or twine and use it as cover up in a stand. By adding more cover, you can help break up your outline. I also like to have multiple stand locations for different wind directions. Out West, whitetails may be easier to see, but they are still the same

My first Western whitetail was a small buck that came in to a doe bleat.

elusive, sharp-eyed, sound-sensitive, wind-checking critters they are everywhere.

I harvested my first Western whitetail early in the season while waiting by a trail near the South Platte River in northeastern Colorado. My stand was in a small, crooked cottonwood tree near a well-used trail. I had watched whitetails through my binoculars pass by this cottonwood on multiple occasions. Usually, it was in the morning when they were traveling to some thick plum thickets to bed down. There were a few farmhouses and a county road close to the small river. Like most areas of the eastern plains in Western states, there was only a small strip of trees that followed the water through the otherwise dry country. The brush and treeline were only about 50 yards wide at most points, and the river ran through the middle of the trees. Outside of the few trees along the river, farm fields and open prairies left little cover for the deer to hide in.

I crawled up into my crooked tree before first light, and only a few hours had passed when the young buck came walking by my stand. My arrow flashed across the 10 yards separating us, and the buck was mine. His little nubs weren't record-book material, but that didn't matter in the least to me. I was proud as punch with my first Western whitetail.

When the rut approaches, bucks start to travel looking for receptive does. They usually follow the fingers of trees and brush found along waterways in the eastern plains. This is when the small strips of cover offer a huge advantage to bowhunters. By sitting all day in a funnel area or by a popular trail, bowhunters can easily find themselves in range of a nice buck.

RATTLING

Just before and during the rut is a good time to try rattling. I prefer to rattle at a buck I can see so that I can gauge his reaction, as opposed to "rattling blind." I have had the best success when rattling at bucks more than 100 yards away. I have spooked bucks by rattling when they were too close. Cover and visibility are big factors here. If you're in open country and a buck can't see the two other bucks that are supposed to be fighting, he will usually get suspicious, so try rattling in cover, or use a decoy.

I start by gently ticking the antler tines and see what the buck does. If he starts coming, I set the antlers down and get ready. If he ignores the sound or just stops and stares for a little while and then moves away, I try rattling again a little more aggressively. I also throw in a couple of grunts as well. Stay alert, because often-times a buck that you never knew was around may slip in. Rattling works only a small percentage of the time. It takes the right buck, the right time of year, and the right set of circumstances for everything to fall into place. When it does work it is exciting. Having a buck charge into your stand is a rush, whether you get a shot or not.

A broken-up whitetail I harvested on a river bottom in eastern Colorado.

CALLING

Whitetails are vocal animals and use a series of different sounds to communicate with each other. They use bleats, snorts, grunts, wheezes, and, of course, the warning blowing and snorting, which is the one we bowhunters are used to hearing. When hunting, I always carry a bleat call and a grunt tube with me. Oftentimes, you can lure a buck within range with a few bleats or a grunt call. I usually bleat or grunt only when I see a buck. I use a two- to three-call sequence, spacing the calls about two to three seconds apart. Whitetails can pinpoint a sound from a long distance, so if the buck reacts to your calls there is rarely any reason to call again. If he starts coming, get ready. Also, be prepared for him to try to circle downwind. I like to try a grunt or bleat on bucks that are close, but are obviously not going to pass by within bow range.

Don't be disappointed if your rattling or calling doesn't cause a reaction—it usually doesn't. As I mentioned earlier, it takes the right deer and the right circumstances. Don't give up on it. Eventually, you will call or rattle to the right buck and it will be one of the highlights of your bowhunting memories.

Tony Pachelli harvested this 180-inch Pope & Young buck from a tree stand near a southern Colorado river bottom.

My wife harvested this big Western whitetail doe from a tree stand in eastern Colorado.

SCRAPES

Since mule deer do not make scrapes, if you are out West and spot a suspicious-looking, pawed-out piece of ground with a branch hanging over it, you've just found yourself a whitetail scrape. Hunting scrapes out West is just like hunting scrapes in the rest of the country. Sometimes hunting one or a series of scrapes pans out, and other times it doesn't. My trail cameras have proven to me that most of the time bucks visit scrapes at night. There are exceptions, and I have seen some real eye-poppers stop to refresh scrapes in the middle of the day. As for me, I will stick with a hot food source, well-used trail, or funnel area before I set up on a scrape. If you're curious what bucks are visiting the scrape or at what times, set up a trail camera. They are great scouting tools that can be used to monitor the scrape when you can't be there.

DECOYS

I have had more success out West in decoying whitetails than mule deer. This doesn't mean it is a cure-all because decoying, like calling, only works occasionally. I prefer to set up where a deer will see the decoy, but not from too far away. I feel that if a deer can see a decoy for too long it becomes suspicious by the lack of move-ment. A moving tail can really add a touch of realism to an otherwise stagnant setup. For decoys, I prefer either a bedded doe or a standing buck. I try to place them in small open pockets or on the edge of a broken field. By avoiding placing decoys where deer can see them a long ways off—say, more than 100 yards—I think you improve your chances of having a deer react positively. I also like to place the decoy 20 to 30 yards upwind of me so that if the deer circles downwind, it will walk by within easy range.

Decoys are also great to use in combination with rattling or calling. By appealing to both his auditory and visual senses, you can increase the odds of a buck charging in.

SCENTS AND CLOTHING

Attractants, scents, and some of the "scent-free" products on the market certainly have some merit. I have used doe estrus-type scents with success in the past. I do feel that their benefits are sometimes exaggerated. Just as calling, rattling, and decoying work only occasionally in certain situations, scents fall into the same category, in my opinion. At the right time of year, with the right buck in the right situation, scents will draw bucks into bow range to investigate.

The most common mistake I see with scents is using too much. Whitetails have sensitive noses. If the scent is going to work, it is best to follow the manufacturer's instructions. One of my favorite ways to use scents is as a sexual attractant. During the rut, when bucks are cruising, I will sometimes make a scent line. For a scent line I use a clean cotton rag tied to a 10-foot piece of string. I place two or three drops of estrus scent on the rag and begin walking toward my tree stand. I may start my drag anywhere from 100 to 300 yards upwind of my stand. Every 50 yards or so, I will place one or two more drops on the rag. My theory here is that the scent will get stronger as the buck follows it toward my stand. I then leave the rag about 10 yards upwind from my stand, either in a low bush or partially covered by leaves. You must be careful not to touch any brush while walking in, and I advise wearing rubber boots and clean clothing to keep your human scent to a minimum.

These whitetails seem perfectly at home out West.

Products such as scent-free clothing, soaps, shampoos, gums, deodorants, and sprays are all designed to help mask or hide your scent. In my opinion, it is impossible to totally eliminate human scent. There is no product on the market that will accomplish this. What we can and should do is to try and diminish it as much as possible. I believe that most animals are tuned in to react to different levels of human scent.

I used to hunt a small patch of woods that was only a couple of acres. There were two houses close by, with the nearest being about 100 yards from my stand. That ranch house constantly had people coming in and out of it, from farmhands to friends of the kids who lived there. The wind was generally from the northwest, where the house was. I could constantly smell smoke from their fire, and even bacon on some mornings.

The deer that called that small woodlot home were used to human scent and noise. One would surmise, then, that human scent wouldn't alarm them. Not so. One morning, I was sitting in my stand within plain view of the house, and a young doe was crossing the creek downwind of me. When she hit my wind, she threw her head up, looked in my direction, and bolted into the brush. I would have called it a fluke if not for the fact that every time I got winded, the deer would react similarly. That was almost 20 years ago now, and I firmly believe that deer operate on levels of scent.

In most areas, deer and other game are constantly bombarded with scents from our world. They have learned to react like a smoke alarm. I have one in my house, and if I burn something just a little bit and a little smoke drifts around the house and everyone can smell it, the alarm doesn't go off. But, if I really burn something and a lot of smoke fills the air, then the alarm is triggered to emit a high-pitched, irritating noise. Deer and other animals have thresholds as well. As bowhunters, we can gain an advantage by reducing our scent to the point that it does not set off the alarm. This is where clean rubber boots, keeping yourself clean, and hanging your clothes outside or storing them in plastic bags can help. Many of the scent-free products and clothing can also help you diminish your scent—but there is no magic solution. Your best bet is to always stay downwind. However, if by minimizing your scent you can harvest an animal that otherwise would have busted you, then I say it was worth the effort.

FIELD-JUDGING WHITE-TAILED DEER

It takes 125 inches after deductions to make the Pope & Young record book for a typical white-tailed deer. As with all species, any whitetail you take with a bow is a trophy, but for those looking for an above-average buck here is a quick way to rough-gauge whether or not you're looking at a record-book buck.

First, check that your buck has a minimum of four points on each side. Only a handful of six-point bucks (Eastern count) have ever made the minimum, so at least an eight-point is the first thing I look for. Next, add up the points in inches on one side, not counting the main beam. So for an eight-point you would add the G-1,

G-2, and G-3. If they add up to 21 inches or more and the other side is symmetrical, shoot him. Odds are he will make minimum unless his main beam, width measurement, or circumference measurements are unusually small. Since all you usually have is a few seconds, this is a good quick reference for deciding if the buck is a shooter. There is no substitute for experience. The more you practice judging whitetails on your friends' walls, or in the local sporting goods shop, the better you will get.

Rob Lucero took this beautiful Pope & Young whitetail in southern Colorado by using the spot-and-stalk method.

FACTS ABOUT WHITE-TAILED DEER (*Odocoileus virginianus*)

The name whitetail comes from the long white hair found on the underside of the deer's tail. The white hair is obvious and looks like a white flag when the tail is held erect. This usually happens when the deer are frightened, nervous, or running from danger. Only the bucks have antlers, which they grow every year in the spring and shed near the end of winter.

Their lifespan is nine years, but this number is misleading since predation and hunting pressure often reduce the actual average lifespan to one-and-one-half to two-and-one-half years.

Weight varies according to regions and food sources, but most whitetail bucks average 150 to 300 pounds, while the smaller does average 100 to 175 pounds. The fawns are born spotted and they gradually lose their spots by fall.

White-tailed deer are extremely agile and great jumpers, easily clearing 8-foot-high fences. They can reach speeds of up to 40 miles per hour and have extremely acute senses of smell, hearing, and eyesight, which they use to avoid predators. Whitetails are territorial and usually live out their lives in a small home range.

Besides using vocalizations to communicate, whitetails have scent glands between their hooves on all four feet, as well as tarsal glands on the inside of their hind legs at the hocks. They also have preorbital glands in front of their eyes that the bucks often rub to leave scent posts. Scents from these glands are used to communicate everything from health to sexual readiness.

The does usually come into heat in late October to early November for a 24- to 30-hour period. If a doe is not mated successfully during this time, she will come back into heat again approximately 28 days later. Does that are not pregnant that come back into heat in early December trigger another flurry of buck movement, commonly referred to as the second rut. This cycle will often repeat again if a doe is not bred.

The rut is one of the most popular times for bowhunters to try to harvest a buck. Give western whitetail hunting a chance. If you're lucky and harvest a deer, try my favorite recipe.

A whitetail fawn I walked up on.

This buck doesn't even seem to be trying hard to clear the fence.

WHITETAIL MEDALLIONS WITH BACON AND PARSLEY SAUCE

Allow 6–8 ounces per serving
    Deer backstrap
    1 cup flour
    1 pound bacon
    2 cups chopped fresh parsley
    1 stick butter
    Salt and pepper to taste

Fry the entire pound of bacon, reserve the fat, and break bacon into 1-inch pieces and set aside. Slice backstrap into 1/2-inch-thick medallions. Coat medallions with flour and fry in reserved bacon fat until medium to medium rare. Place on a platter. Place butter and parsley into a medium saucepan and cook over medium heat until parsley is wilted in the butter, approximately 5 minutes. Season parsley mixture with salt and pepper to taste. Pour parsley mixture over medallions and place bacon pieces on top.

7
MOUNTAIN LION

Mountain lion, catamount, zephyr, cougar, panther, painter, and puma are just a few of the many names given to the largest cat in North America. This amazing animal tops the charts as one of the most efficient, powerful, and elusive predators anywhere. Found in large numbers in all the Western states and in more states in the East than many people realize, the mountain lion is rarely seen. Its reclusive nature and primarily nocturnal habits, combined with its sharp senses, make this cat the true "ghost of the woods."

Mountain lions are big, beautiful killers.

Though they were previously thought to harvest only sick or weak prey, research has proven that mountain lions routinely harvest healthy big game animals as large as mature bull elk. Although their diet varies and includes a myriad of small game animals, deer are their mainstay. A recent study by the University of Wyoming, conducted in conjunction with the Wyoming Cooperative Fish and Wildlife Research Unit, confirmed what most lion hunters already knew. The study found that, on average, a lion kills a deer or elk every seven days! That means that one lion is capable of killing 52 deer or elk a year.

Unfortunately, it is very difficult for biologists to estimate lion populations accurately. Every Western biologist I have spoken to in several states assured me that the lion populations were very healthy, but could not give me hard numbers. The Colorado Game and Fish Commission has estimated that there are "between three thousand to seven thousand mountain lions, with four thousand five hundred to five thousand five hundred most likely." Therefore, if we assume that there are only 3,000 lions in Colorado, with each taking one deer or elk a week, that is 156,000 deer or elk per year lost to lion predation alone. What is even more interesting is that the majority of the deer kills I find are bucks. It makes sense when you think about it. Bucks are often alone, and it is easier to sneak up on one pair of eyes than multiple pairs of eyes.

To put into perspective what amazing hunters lions are, just think of how wary their primary prey (deer and elk) are. Then imagine what it takes to consistently stalk them and jump onto their backs, killing them with a quick bite to the back of the neck.

A client's big tom and the dogs that treed him.

My fascination with lions began when I met the late Rob Pedretti. Rob was a houndsman and guide in southern Colorado. He took me out on my first lion hunt, and I was hooked. A wild mountain lion is something few people ever see, and once you have seen one it is something you will never forget. Rob had treed more than 250 lions with his self-trained hounds. He was the most knowledgeable lion hunter I had ever met. He had a true respect for the cats he pursued and a love for the hounds that helped him. Rob asked me to be his partner soon after my first lion hunt, and I got to learn from the best. We treed 18 lions for clients together before he turned me loose on my own. I also became addicted to the sound of baying hounds and went on to train some of my own dogs, which I use for my clients on guided mountain lion hunts.

Since that first lion hunt, I have learned a great deal about lions and their habits. I am still constantly amazed by these big cats. In December 2004, I saw firsthand something that made me realize what amazing predators lions are. While looking for tracks on a ranch not far from my house, I crossed a large lion track in the snow. I followed its tracks across a small ridge and into some thick oak brush dotted with pines. The tracks soon changed from those of a walking lion to one that was hunting. The paw tracks were close together, and one just in front of the other. The tracks also showed where the lion had crouched down in the snow every few yards.

I could tell that the lion was hunting something, but I had no idea what it was. I followed the stalking cat tracks to a small pine tree, directly behind which the cat had lain down. Large dig marks indicated that the cat had sprung from its crouched location. I looked, but even in the fresh snow I couldn't find any more lion tracks. There in the snow in front of me were two fresh elk beds. Both elk had burst out of their beds running.

One elk bed had a pile of hair in it, and the cat tracks were gone. It took me a minute to realize that the lion had leaped onto the back of one of the elk that had been bedded there just hours before I arrived. I followed the scrambling elk track in the snow. My adrenaline was pumping full tilt, and I remember stopping for a few moments to try to calm down. When I started down the elk track again, I started finding clumps of elk hair and specks of blood on the snow. The elk had run through some thick oak brush, popping off limbs as it ran. Obviously the elk was trying to dislodge the cat from its back. The elk track ended about 100 yards from its bed in a pile of blood and a drag mark.

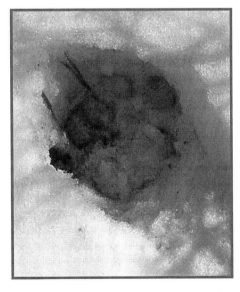

A good example. Here this cat appears to have five toes. It actually just put its rear paw in exactly the same place as its front paw, giving the appearance of an extra toe.

I followed the drag mark almost 50 yards to a huge, 6 x 6 bull. Just imagine the power it takes to kill an elk. Then think of the strength it must have taken to drag a dead bull 50 yards! I tried to move the dead bull but could hardly budge him. The lion had already consumed most of one front shoulder on the bull. The cat tracks running away in the snow confirmed that I had just scared the cat off its kill. I ran to the top of the ridge and called my good friend and guide Jake Kraus. I told him to get our client and which dogs to bring. He met me at the scene with our client, Wayne Ireland. They were both as amazed as I was with the scene that could easily be recreated by looking at the fresh tracks.

Jake and I released the dogs, and within 30 minutes we could hear the hounds baying. The large cat had a belly full of fresh elk meat and did not travel far before treeing in a large ponderosa pine. Jake captured the whole hunt on video, including Wayne making a great shot with his longbow. Seconds after the arrow connected, the big tom was down.

After we harvested the lion that killed the bull, I called two local game wardens to come have a look. Since both men are outdoorsmen, they were also impressed with both the cat and the bull elk and the awesome life-and-death struggle that had taken place. One explained that he had seen other large bulls that lions had killed and shared my admiration for these big cats. The rack off that bull is now one of my favorite trophies and reminds me of what efficient hunters mountain lions are.

TRACKS AND CAT SIZE

The key to being successful on a mountain lion hunt is finding a track and being able to determine accurately how large the cat is and how old the track is. Weather conditions are the next major factor. Let's take them one at a time.

The size of the cat is a

Guide Tony Pachelli looking at some mountain lion tracks in the snow. Notice how the cat stepped on the rock. (Remember that a cat usually puts its rear paw in the same track as its front paw, so what you're actually looking at is the track from the hind foot.)

tough one. Ask around and you will usually get a lot of different answers. In my opinion, the best way to know you're on a large or small cat is to measure the cat's stride.

When lions walk, they usually place each hind foot in the same track as their front foot on the same side. So you are most likely looking at the track of the hind foot. Measuring the stride is the most accurate way to determine the size of the cat. Stride is the distance between one track and another track made by the same foot. (Some people measure this between two tracks on opposite sides, or half stride, which means measuring between the left-side stride and the right side.) This will be shorter than the full-stride measurement, which is measured from the front of one track to the front of the other track on the same side.

A cat that is striding 40 inches or more from the front of one track to the front of the other on the same foot is usually a mature tom, while the strides of females and younger male cats usually measure less than 35 inches. Deep snow, inclines, or declines will reduce the stride measurement. Bear in mind that you want to measure a walking stride. You can be misled by measuring a running cat or one that is stalking.

Note: I was always taught to measure stride from the front of one track to the front of the other, or the rear of one track to the rear of the other on the same side. Strides on animals are often measured toe to toe, since animals usually put the front of their paw or hoof down first, whereas people's strides are usually measured from heel to heel, since we put our heels down first when walking. Though there are several ways to measure stride, this method has always worked for me.

Mountain lion tracks show four toes, and the claws rarely show unless the cat is climbing or trying to grip on a slick surface.

AGING A TRACK

Aging a track takes practice. The best way to learn is by watching a track age under different weather conditions. Shade, sun, temperature, moisture, dirt, mud, wind, and snow are just a few factors that must be taken into consideration when trying to guess the age of a track. Tracks in a single string can be in different conditions, depending on where they are. I have started on tracks that looked fresh in the shade or deep

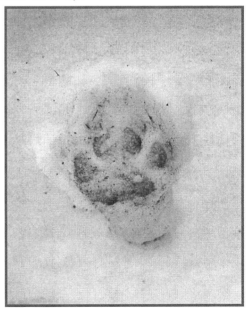

Here is an older track that has thawed and refrozen at least once.

snow, but that looked old where the sun or wind had deteriorated the quality of the tracks, even though they were made by the same cat, often within minutes of each other.

One simple thing that can help in aging a track is knowing the weather. For example, I once found a set of cat tracks in about 4 inches of snow early one morning crossing a road. The track looked fresh and had not been melted or frozen. Since I knew that the weather had been relatively warm the day before, and that the temperature had not dipped to below freezing until about 10 o'clock that night, it was easy to surmise that the track had been made sometime between 10 p.m. the night before and 6 a.m. when I found the track. Had it been made earlier, the track would have been in damp, wet snow and the track would have been frozen once the temperature dropped below freezing.

I was guiding Bruce Cull (president of the National Field Archery Association) that morning, and Jake Kraus was also with me looking for tracks. I showed Bruce the track and told him I felt confident that the track had been made within the last eight hours. We turned the dogs loose and after following the dog's tracks a few miles we topped a ridge and could hear the dogs baying in the valley below us.

As we quietly slipped up to the tree, we could see the tom lying on a limb growling and watching the hounds below him. Jake and I eased underneath the cat and leashed up the dogs. This is a safety measure to keep the dogs from attacking a dying or wounded cat as it comes out of the tree. Bruce made a textbook shot, and his first mountain lion was on the ground in seconds.

Bruce Cull of South Dakota with the Pope & Young tom the hounds treed.

WEATHER CONDITIONS

On a lion hunt, good weather conditions are extremely important. Good conditions usually mean a fresh blanket of snow in which to look for lion tracks. Fresh snow makes tracks easier to find and easier to age, and makes it easier for the dogs to pick up the scent of the lion. No snow makes it more difficult to find tracks, more difficult to age the tracks, and more difficult for the dogs to follow the scent. Some outfitters who hunt in areas that get little or no snow have hounds that excel in dry-ground trailing. However, if the weather turns hot and dry, even the best dogs can't follow the scent. So when you go on your lion hunt, remember that there is no guarantee. It is usually the persistent hunter and guide who get to see the most impressive cat in North America.

A big tom in a tree.

FIELD-JUDGING MOUNTAIN LIONS

The best bet is to trust your guide on the size and sex of the cat. In all states that currently allow mountain lion hunting, you can harvest both males and females. As I mentioned earlier, the cat's stride is a good way to determine the size and sex. Once the cat is in a tree or bayed up on the ground, you can look at the overall size of the cat. Another good indicator is to look 4 to 5 inches under the anus of the cat if possible. Males will have a small black spot of hair about an inch in diameter. For a cat to make the Pope & Young record book, it must score a minimum of 13 ⁵⁄₁₆ inches, which is the measurement of the combined length and width of the skull. An experienced lion hunter can usually guess the cat pretty closely by looking at its head. If the ears are more than 5 inches apart at the base, it is probably a contender for the record book.

FACTS ABOUT MOUNTAIN LIONS (*Felis concolor*)

Mountain lions have an average lifespan of 9 to 12 years in the wild. A female can have as many as six kittens in a litter, but usually only two survive to adulthood. Kittens are born with spots that fade within eight months to a year. The female raises the kittens and teaches them to hunt. The male's only role is conception. Occasionally, the young lions will stay with their mother for as long as 18 months before leaving and finding their own territory.

Here is the big bull the cat killed and my client Wayne Ireland of Maine and his trophy cat.

Mountain lions are usually solitary animals, although on occasion littermates will hunt together into adulthood. Cats have their own distinct territories that vary in size based on the availability of prey species. During the winter, cats will often migrate to follow game into different areas. When forced together due to prey animals being concentrated in only one area, mountain lions practice what biologists refer to as mutual avoidance, coming together only to breed or fight in territorial disputes.

Unlike many other predators, mountain lions only like fresh meat they have killed themselves. Only in rare circumstances will a lion eat carrion or feed off another animal's kill.

Adult males can be more than 8 feet in length from their nose to the tip of their tail. On average, adult males weigh between 130 to 160 pounds. Adult females can be 7 feet long and on average weigh between 70 and 110 pounds.

EQUIPMENT SUGGESTIONS

Since only a handful of lions have ever been harvested without dogs, odds are your cat will be treed by a trained pack of hounds. Shots are usually close, and it's rare to shoot over 25 yards. Cats are not difficult to kill, and 9 to 12 inches of penetration will go completely through the chest cavity. Razor-sharp broadheads—as always—are a must. I suggest a minimum of 40 pounds of bow weight for lions.

You may be covering a lot of miles in thick brush, so I advise a lightweight bow. Recurves and longbows work great. I prefer an attached bow quiver, because a side quiver or back quiver can be difficult to maneuver in thick brush.

It is always best to be prepared physically and mentally for any hunt. If you're planning a lion hunt, that goes double. Most lion country is rough, and long, hard

When hunting mountain lions, weather conditions can be harsh. Be prepared with emergency equipment.

hikes are the norm. If you're a flatlander or a mountain dweller in poor shape, be sure to get in shape before heading afield. Climbing stadium steps with a pack is a great way to prepare. Slow and steady is usually the ticket when lion hunting. Don't assume that your guide will have emergency gear. Since lion hunting is often in remote country, take a daypack with fire starter, extra food, water, extra clothes, and a compass or GPS unit. It is always better to have it and not need it than to need it and not have it!

Mountain lions are incredible animals, and once you've seen your first one up close, it is a memory you will never forget.

MOUNTAIN LION BACKSTRAP WITH APPLES AND BLUEBERRY JAM

Note: Mountain lion is much like pork, and almost any pork recipe will work.

Serves 4
    One 2-pound mountain lion backstrap
    3 Granny Smith apples, peeled and cut into ?-inch slices
    ½ cup brown sugar
    ½ stick butter
    ½ cup water
    3 tablespoons olive oil
    Salt and pepper
    One jar of blueberry jam

In a large frying pan, heat 2 tablespoons of olive oil on high heat. Salt and pepper backstrap, then place in pan and sear and brown all sides of the backstrap. Remove from the pan and cover with aluminum foil and bake in a 375-degree oven for one hour until done.

In the meantime, sauté apples for five minutes in 1 tablespoon olive oil, ½ stick of butter, and brown sugar. Add water until apples have a soft texture and the butter and brown sugar have thickened.

When the backstrap is done, slice onto a serving platter, surround with apples, and serve with warm blueberry jam on the side.

8

GUIDED HUNTS:
HOW TO CHOOSE AN OUTFITTER

If you aren't concerned about choosing the right outfitter to take you hunting, you should be. I have spoken with several high-profile bowhunters who spend a lot of time and money with outfitters, and all reported at least one really bad experience.

For any bowhunter who is thinking about going on a guided hunt, deciding whom to book your hunt with is one of the toughest questions to answer. It is a hard question for a number of very valid reasons. First, outfitted or guided hunts cost a lot of money. Second, we want to avoid a bad or dangerous experience if at all possible. Finally, we all have hopes of bringing home an animal.

Unless they have a close friend who has had a good experience with a particular outfitter, most bowhunters are in the dark when it comes to choosing where to spend their hard-earned money.

Although nothing can guarantee a good experience, we as consumers can and should do research and ask questions that will help us avoid a bad experience. Listed below are important things to consider or ask about before booking your hunt. They will help you make an informed decision on where to go.

Are your guides familiar with bowhunting? Are they bowhunters themselves? Do they understand your range limitations? These are all important questions.

ARE THEY EXPERIENCED IN GUIDING BOWHUNTERS?

This is more important than many people realize! Unfortunately, most hunting outfitters aren't experienced when it comes to bowhunting. Fortunately, there are some excellent archery outfitters and guides out there. It is our job to be sure we are going with an experienced outfitter. I like to ask if the guide who will be taking me is a bowhunter. Oftentimes, rifle guides really don't understand bowhunting or the range limitations and different hunting methods associated with bowhunting. A stand or blind that might be great for a rifle or muzzleloader hunter may be a terrible spot for a bowhunter.

WHAT IS THE GUIDE-TO-HUNTER RATIO?

In other words, will it be one-on-one, or will you be sharing your guide with another hunter? It is worth knowing before you go. If your hunt isn't a one-on-one guided hunt, talk to the outfitter. Some outfitters will offer a one-on-one hunt for a higher fee.

HOW MUCH WILL I SPEND, INCLUDING LICENSES?

Make sure that there are no hidden costs. Get in writing a list of all costs, including license fees or additional transportation costs. Are meals provided? Is there a kill fee? How will I get my meat and trophy home if I harvest an animal? I was once on a caribou hunt where I was on a tight budget. It wasn't until after I'd harvested a caribou that I learned that there was an additional $300 charge to fly it out of camp. Asking ahead of time can save you and the outfitter an unpleasant experience.

Can I stay longer if I need to? Sometimes a few extra days makes all the difference.

HOW MANY DAYS IS THE HUNT?

Does that include travel days? Most guided hunts out West are five to seven days, however, a lot of high-end hunts (over $8,000) can be seven to ten days.

CAN I ADD DAYS IF NOT SUCCESSFUL?

Some outfitters will allow hunters to extend their trip on a pay-per-day basis. Find out if this is possible, and the cost. This is a huge one for me.

Since you have already invested your money and time getting to camp, one or two extra days may be all you need to get a shot at the animal you are after. Weather can also knock a few days off a hunt in a hurry. Bring this up ahead of time. It may save your trip.

HOW PHYSICAL IS THE HUNT?

Obviously, physical ability varies from person to person, as do the requirements of different hunts and terrains. Even a hunter who is totally out of shape can easily walk 100 yards from a truck to a tree stand, whereas an elk or lion hunt will demand a totally different set of requirements. How much walking will we be doing on average? How much stand hunting? Will we be using horses? If the answer is yes, and you're not comfortable on horseback, you may want to look elsewhere.

WHAT PERCENTAGE OF BOWHUNTERS HARVEST THEIR INTENDED SPECIES? AND HOW MANY HAVE OPPORTUNITIES?

Ask for specific numbers. How many bowhunters did you take last year for elk? Of those, how many harvested elk? How many had shot opportunities? In fairness to the outfitter, I like to ask about shot opportunities, not necessarily numbers harvested. Also bear in mind that sometimes a low success rate may be due to bad weather, or inexperienced or out-of-shape hunters. Try to feel out the guide or outfitter so you understand why the success rate is high or low.

Or are you only going to shoot if it is a trophy?

CAN YOU SEND ME REFERENCES?

Most outfitters have a prepared reference list. Of course, most reference lists are filled with hunters who had an enjoyable time and harvested animals. Ask for a list of specific references, including names and contact information. If possible, ask for references from hunters in your state who have hunted with the outfitter. Be sure to ask for references from bowhunters who hunted the same area you will be in, or at least hunted the same species you are planning to hunt. Talking to other bowhunters can often give you a good feel for what to expect, from terrain to guides. Ask for references from hunters who have not harvested as well. Sometimes your best information will come from these guys.

HAVE YOU HAD ANY GAME VIOLATIONS?

It is good to know if you will be hunting with someone who is a legal and ethical outfitter. I suggest calling the game officer in the region you will be hunting. If the game officer advises against the outfitter, I wouldn't go.

DO YOU HUNT PRIVATE OR PUBLIC LAND?

This is just a good FYI. Some public land areas are great, and outfitters will usually charge more to hunt private ranches. Do you have exclusive hunting rights? How much property do you hunt?

Ask any other questions that you may be concerned about, such as the type of food served or lodging, if that concerns you. Ask for a suggested "to bring" list. These are handy and let you know what equipment the outfitter expects you to bring. Try to have all these questions in order when you call an outfitter—that way you can have them all answered at once and save you both valuable time. I always try to compare two to five outfitters for each species I am going after. That way I can compare notes and prices.

Where will I be staying? You may want to know.

As a hunter, I have booked a lot of hunts for different species. I have found that most of my bad experiences have come from outfitters with whom I have not communicated very much. I have also had some tremendous experiences with outfitters that will provide me with fond memories for the rest of my life. And while some of these great memories include harvesting an animal, many of them did not.

THE OTHER SIDE OF THE COIN

As a full-time outfitter who guides ten months a year for antelope, bear, elk, mule deer, turkey, and mountain lion, I have guided clients on successful trips for all these species. I have also guided hunters on unsuccessful trips for all of them. Sometimes I screwed up. At other times, the weather prevented us from being successful. Sometimes my client's mistakes caused them to go home empty-handed. And sometimes the animals just didn't cooperate.

Below are some tips from an outfitter/guide's point of view that will help you have a more successful and enjoyable experience.

BE HONEST ABOUT YOUR CONDITION

If you tell the outfitter that you're in great shape and can go all day, you may very well be sent into an area that requires that. If you are overweight or have any disabilities or handicaps, explain this to the outfitter. Many outfitters can accommodate people with disabilities or handicaps.

BE AWARE OF YOUR RANGE LIMITATIONS

The effective range for each bowhunter varies. Try to be honest and accurate in your assessment of how far you are comfortable shooting. Once a range is stated, don't be surprised if you're asked to shoot that distance. All my guides, myself included, like to see our clients shoot before we take them out. It gives us an idea of what range they're comfortable with. Other outfitters with whom I have hunted usually do the same thing.

SHOW UP READY

Bowhunting is a physical endeavor. Try to be in the best shape possible for any hunt. Be sure to practice with and know the equipment you will be bringing. You're better off bringing the old bow you are comfortable with rather than buying a brand new one just before a trip. (It happens.)

TRUST YOUR GUIDE (Very Important)

You have already made your decision and paid your money. Don't question the guide. If you're not prepared to be guided, don't go on a guided hunt. A lot of animals have taken the trail back to their beds because of hunters not following their guide's instructions. Are guides always right? Of course not. But if you did your research, odds are he knows more about the animal and the terrain you are hunting in than you do.

TO SHOOT OR PASS?

This is a tough one. I advise hunters who are trophy hunting to have a clear idea of the animal they will be happy with. I also usually suggest that hunters harvest an animal on the first day of the hunt that they would be happy with on the last day of the hunt. Many hunters, including myself, have passed on animals early in a hunt that we later wished we had harvested.

TIPS

The accepted and often published rate for tips is 10 to 15 percent of the cost of your hunt. Most guides, like waitresses, survive on the tips they make. If a guide doesn't do a good job, don't tip him. If you think he did an exceptional job, tip him more. If multiple guides took you, either split up the tip accordingly or ask the outfitter to divvy it up. If you have a cook preparing your meals, I suggest a tip of $10 a day.

Shoot or pass? It's your decision.

ATTITUDE

The old adage about one bad apple holds true in hunting camps. No one, including the other hunters and guides, wants to spend time with someone who has a bad attitude. Most true bowhunters I know are optimists. You have to be one to be a bowhunter. So bring your best attitude to camp, because another adage about your success being in the hands of your guide is also true.

Lastly, I would like to mention that when you purchase a fair-chase hunt from any outfitter you are buying an opportunity to hunt. You are in no way purchasing an animal. When you choose to hunt five days to two weeks for a wild animal with any weapon, you must always be aware that you may come home empty-handed. Even outfitters who claim to be 99 percent successful have sent at least one person home without an animal.

So be sure to enjoy every sunrise and sunset, as well as the people and the terrain, because that is really why we are all out there anyway. If you don't lose sight of that, you will never have an unsuccessful trip.

9

HOW TO PURCHASE OR DRAW TAGS OUT WEST

Before choosing where out West to hunt and for what species, you should take a lot of things into consideration. For example, some states have licenses available over the counter in certain areas for specific species. Others have lottery systems in place for tags, where it is the luck of the draw that dictates whether you will be hunting or not. Most Western states also have a preference point system set up for hunters who apply for tags. For every year you don't draw a tag, you get a preference point. Hunters with the most preference points are drawn first for areas with only a limited number of tags available. Be sure to check the regulations for the state or states you are interested in hunting. Request any information they have on number of tags given out in different areas, and the odds on drawing for those tags. Also, check hunter success ratios. In today's world of computers, with just a few hours of research you can find out what states have the best success rates in which areas. You can also figure out what the odds are of drawing.

Some states have different regulations for the same species, based on which part of the state you want to hunt.

Sometimes you have to play the game. For example, while researching Rocky Mountain goat tags in Colorado, I realized that the odds of drawing a rifle tag were higher than the odds of drawing an archery tag. I wanted to hunt with my bow, but I also wanted to put in for a tag I had the best odds of drawing. I put in for a rifle tag and drew. I took my bow during a rifle season and harvested a beautiful goat. Without checking the statistics, I may still be putting in for that tag.

I harvested this Rocky Mountain goat on a public land backpacking hunt. After years of putting in for an archery tag, I learned that I could increase my odds of drawing by applying for a rifle tag and hunting with a bow!

Check the regulations! In some states and for certain seasons, you must hunt with the weapon that corresponds with the same season you applied for. To make it even more confusing, some limited-draw tags are not weapon-specific, meaning you can use whatever is legal in that state. Another time that checking drawing odds helped me out was on a Shiras moose tag in Wyoming. I had been putting in for a few years and decided to check the odds of drawing a bull tag for the unit I was applying for. When I saw that the odds were less than 10 percent, I looked into the odds of drawing a cow tag. To my surprise, they were 100 percent! I applied for and drew a cow tag. I got to enjoy a great hunt in Wyoming, where I harvested a huge cow moose with my bow. For me, this trumped waiting another six to eight years to have even a reasonable chance at drawing a bull tag.

I applied for and drew a Wyoming cow moose tag after learning that my odds of drawing a bull tag were going to be pretty slim for five more years.

Chris Parrino of Illinois put in for and drew a limited tag for archery mule deer. He shot this buck with me the first evening of his hunt. By drawing limited tags, you increase your odds of hunting in less-pressured, high-quality areas.

When researching, decide whether you are more interested in a trophy animal or an opportunity at any animal. Most of the limited-draw or trophy units may take a few years to draw. However, when you do finally draw that tag, if you have done your research, you will be hunting in prime country with little pressure from other hunters. Although these limited-draw or trophy areas have their advantages, there are still great trophy opportunities on public land areas out West where tags can be purchased over the counter. You just may have to do a little legwork to find them.

The best thing you can do for yourself is spend a little time researching where to go. Some of my best leads on both public land, do-it-yourself hunts and guided hunts have come from friends who have already been on such a hunt. Another quick and easy way to get some info is to call a local game warden or biologist in the area you are interested in. You will probably be surprised at how willing most game wardens and biologists are to help people who call them. Getting in touch with them is pretty easy. Just call the main fish and game office or whatever regulatory agency manages the hunting. Ask for a field officer or biologist who could help a nonresident with some questions on hunting. Mention the species you are interested in, so they can choose the best person for you to speak with. Most of the people I have spoken with are outdoorsmen and more than willing to divulge some great information.

Another option is to hire a service to do your research. There are several companies that research success ratios and odds of drawing for every big game species in all states, and for a nominal fee they will even apply for the tags for you. Since states all have different deadlines, this can be a quick and easy way of increasing your odds of drawing a tag in a limited-draw area. The two I have used in the past are Carter's Hunter Services (www.huntinfool.com) and Western Hunter (www.westernhunter.com).

This bighorn ewe tag was another public land backpacking hunt. I could have waited years and hoped to draw a ram tag. Instead, I enjoyed a great self-guided hunt. There is nothing wrong with holding out for trophy animals in hard-to-draw units—just figure out what floats your boat and start researching and putting in for tags. The sooner you start applying, the quicker that letter saying "successful applicant" will hit your mailbox.

10
HOW NOT TO GET LOST

hen I first spotted the bowhunter, I was a little bummed out. It was only about an hour before dark, and I had been expecting to see elk, not a bowhunter. I had backpacked into the area and thought I was totally alone. My friend Blye Chadwick and I trapped this area in the winter for pine marten, and we had never seen anyone this far back in the wilderness in years past. The guy was walking fast through the small meadow when I stepped out of the timber to say Hi. Upon seeing me, he ran up and asked if I knew where the road was. Apparently he had gotten turned around that morning and had been walking all day trying to find the road he and his friend were camped on. After he gave me directions to where his camp was, I realized he had come close to 8 miles in the wrong direction.

I gave him easy directions to another main road that was relatively close by, but he was adamant that I take him to the road myself. As I led him out, I learned that he had no compass, no map, and no emergency gear. Had we not met, he would have surely spent an uncomfortable night in the dark.

Although it's easy for me to chuckle at that story now, I have been that guy on a few occasions myself.

It can happen when you least expect it.

You look around and realize you're not sure how to get back to your camp, truck, house, buddy, downed animal . . .

I am not proud to admit it but I have also hunted without a map, a compass, and emergency gear. Sometimes it was because I felt I knew the area really well and didn't think I would need it. In fact, I used to be proud of the fact that I could get around just fine without a compass. Then I learned a lesson in humility myself.

My most embarrassing lost moment was with a client. It was about 10 years ago and I thought I knew the area pretty well. We hiked about three miles from camp to a small meadow that I knew. Just before dark, my client shot a nice 6 x 6 bull elk with his rifle. After I got done caping the bull and quartering the carcass, it was dark. Since I was carrying a heavy load, I opted for a little different route back to camp where the footing would be a little easier.

After three hours of hard hiking without seeing anything familiar in my flashlight beam, I got a little worried. When I got to the creek that I thought was the one we had crossed coming in, and it was flowing the wrong way, I knew I was turned around. Fortunately, I did know the main road was down the mountain a few miles, so I turned and headed down the mountain. Finally arriving at the road, we lucked into a camp of hunters who were kind enough to drive us around the mountain. We finally arrived at our camp at close to 1 a.m., and I vowed to never let that happen to me again.

I now carry a compass with me all the time, usually accompanied by a map of the area I am in.

TOPOGRAPHIC MAPS

As bowhunters, we can hunt more efficiently and safely with some basic orientation skills. A topographic map is a huge asset to the bowhunter. The best-known "topo" maps are published by the United States Geological Survey (USGS). Topo maps show large-scale detail and a multidimensional likeness of the land's surface. They graphically represent the physical features of a place or region. Topo maps are easy to get your hands on. You can purchase a topographic map for any region in the country by going to Web sites such as www.usgs.gov or www.topozone.com.

You can also purchase topographic map software for your computer, such as TOPO!, published by the National Geographic Society (www.nationalgeographic.com), or Topo USA, published by DeLorme (www.delorme.com). Many outdoor specialty stores also carry topographic maps that you can purchase.

To properly read or understand a topo map, you must learn the symbols used and their meaning. Elevation and contour are represented by brown lines called contour lines. These contour lines connect points of equal elevation. Not every contour line is labeled with an elevation value. However, with the known values found in various locations on topo maps, you can easily count the lines up or down from the known elevation line and add or subtract the designated contour interval to figure out elevation. The contour interval, or CI, is printed at the bottom of all topo maps below the scale. The CI represents the difference between two contour lines. The most common CIs are 20 or 40 feet. When contour lines make small circles, they represent the peak or top of a hill or a mountain. Contour lines close together represent a steep slope. Contour lines merging represent a cliff. A large gap between contour lines indicates a shallow slope. The absence of contour lines represents flat areas unchanging in elevation. Topo maps show water, usually represented in blue, and also show creeks, rivers, lakes, and even small ponds that hold water. This is obviously

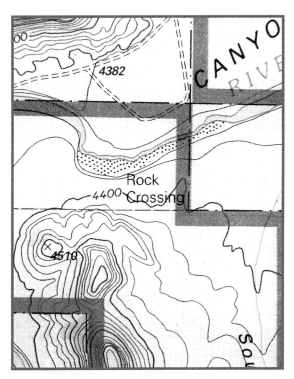

Notice all the contour lines just south west of Rock Crossing. This is showing an increase in elevation. The elevation near the "C" in Crossing is 4,400 feet. The contour lines show an incline that goes up to 4,510 feet, marked at 20-foot intervals.

very beneficial for the bowhunter to be aware of, especially in dry regions of the West, where any water is extremely important.

Once you understand how to properly read a topo map, you can recognize valleys, meadows, trees, and everything else on the earth's surface for the area your

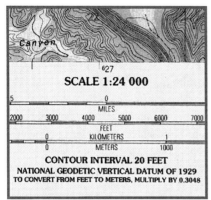

SCALE 1:24 000

CONTOUR INTERVAL 20 FEET
NATIONAL GEODETIC VERTICAL DATUM OF 1929
TO CONVERT FROM FEET TO METERS, MULTIPLY BY 0.3048

On the bottom of topo maps, you will find the scale that the map is in and the contour interval. This map's CI is 20 feet.

map covers. Imagine being able to pick a great funnel area just from looking at a map of an area you have never actually been to. Distances on the map are easily discerned by measuring against the scale. The map's scale is found at the bottom of the map. Bear in mind that distance is measured as the crow flies and does not take into account broken terrain (mountains, valleys, ravines, and so on). So when I am considering how long it will take me to travel somewhere, I follow this rough guide. On even terrain, most people walk about 4 miles per hour. Cut that in half for rough terrain, and you will be in the ballpark of your estimated travel time.

Now that you have a snapshot of what a topographic map is and what it can show you, let's look at what you can do with a compass. Later, we will look at what you can do with a compass and a topo map.

COMPASS

My dictionary defines a compass as "a device used to determine geographical direction, usually consisting of a magnetic needle horizontally mounted or suspended and free to pivot until aligned with the magnetic field of the earth." For me, it is a security blanket. When I have a compass I never really feel lost, even in a blinding snowstorm when I may have no idea which direction the road is. By gosh, I know which way I am walking.

Compasses have a small flaw. They don't know where the road is, either. So it is important when using just a compass to have some idea of where you are going (a bearing) or to keep track of which way you are walking (direction of travel), so you can return to where you started from. By carefully recording the magnetic bearing you're walking, as well as the amount of time or distance traveled at that bearing or other bearings traveled, you can plot a course to retrace your steps. This method, although effective, is time-consuming. Note: Make sure when you are using your compass that there is no metal close by. Your magnetized needle can be pulled off course by placing or holding it in close proximity to a knife, gun barrel, metal bow riser, belt buckle, etc.

When I am bowhunting or scouting, I want to be bowhunting or scouting, not counting my steps or timing how long I have walked on one compass bearing. Therefore, in my opinion the best option is to use a compass in conjunction with a topo map. Now we can easily travel to any point on the map.

Before striking off, however, there are a few more things you need to know.

The first is that your compass does not point to true north (TN). Although there is a lot of technical jargon explaining all this, suffice it to say that your compass points to what is called magnetic north (MN), not true north (TN), which is the North Pole. Without getting overly detailed, to properly follow a map with a compass you must allow for this difference between true north (the North Pole) and magnetic north (where your compass is point-ing). This is called declination. In the Western United States, the

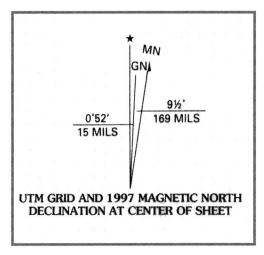

UTM GRID AND 1997 MAGNETIC NORTH DECLINATION AT CENTER OF SHEET

A close-up of the declination diagram. This map is show-ing a declination of 9½ degrees east.

declination between TN and MN is usually between 9 and 17 degrees east. Easterly declinations are often represented by positive values. Fortunately for us, topo maps have a diagram on the bottom showing the declination value for the map's region. TN is represented by a line with a star at the end, and MN is represented by a line with an arrow at the end. They also list GN which stands for Geodetic North, but the only two you need to be concerned with are TN and MN.

It is very important that you correct or adjust to the declination on your map. For example, if your topo map shows a declination of 10 degrees east, then when your compass indicates you are heading at 100 degrees, you are actually heading at 110 degrees. Therefore, if based on your map you want to travel at 100 degrees, you

Two of my compasses. A simple one is on the right. The one on the left has a rotating dial that I can turn to adjust for declination.

must subtract 10 degrees for declination and travel at a 90-degree bearing. Some compasses have a manual adjustment for the degree of declination.

Whether you compensate for declination yourself or adjust the compass, it is very important for accurate travel. If you don't adjust for a declination of 10 degrees (a rough average in the Western states) after walking only 10 miles you would be off by almost two miles. After some practice, you will comfortably be able to travel anywhere on your map. I suggest picking up a map reading book or

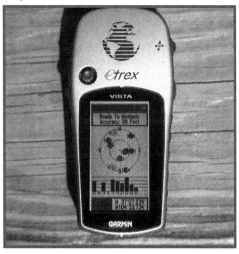

Once the receiver has found the satellites, a GPS unit's navigation accuracy is amazing.

attending a class on topographic map reading. Many specialty outdoor stores offer short introductory classes on orientation skills. It is good to know and will make you a better woodsman who can comfortably find any location with just a compass and a map.

Global Positioning System (GPS) units are rapidly replacing map reading and compass skills as a way to navigate. GPS is a satellite navigation system put into place and controlled by the United States Department of Defense. A GPS is a small, handheld receiver that communicates with satellites that transmit the receiver's location. Amazingly, the accuracy is usually within 20 feet. In other words, if you mark your vehicle in your GPS and walk 10 miles away, your GPS is capable of guiding you back to within 20 feet of your vehicle, or any other marked location.

GPS units have lots of applications that are useful to the bowhunter, including pinpointing your location at any given time, tracking a route so you can follow that exact route back to your starting point, and marking hundreds of specific locations, such as camps, wallows, or tree stands. On certain models, you can also download topo maps for precise navigation in the area where you will be hunting.

I have used my GPS for everything from marking a dead elk to finding a camp in the middle of the night. They are amazing tools and can be a huge asset. I use mine in conjunction with a compass, because when giving you a direction toward a saved or marked position, the GPS gives me the degree you need to head. Instead of leaving my GPS on or constantly checking it every half mile, I simply follow my compass at the heading provided by the GPS.

There are more features too numerous to mention here, so if you are interested in knowing more I suggest researching GPS online. Keep in mind that a GPS is a battery-driven computer that can poop out on you when you need it most. So have an idea of where you are, or better yet carry a topo map and a compass, just in case.

11
BACKPACKING FOR WESTERN GAME ON PUBLIC LAND

ost Western states have vast areas of public land that offer tremendous hunting opportunities. Sometimes finding these game-rich areas can be as simple as getting off the beaten path. Don't get me wrong—occasionally you will find a little gem, a spot close to the road that few people know about and where game is abundant. But that is just not what normally happens. In fact, most public ground access roads and campgrounds get hammered with traffic. I have seen as many as 10 bowhunters within a mile of a popular camping area. Although the high amount of traffic may be discouraging to some hunters, the truth is that most bowhunters don't stray far from their trucks. By doing your research and shouldering a backpack with all you need to live for a week, you can often hike into lightly pressured, almost virgin country within a few miles. Thanks to hauling my gear on my back and camping in remote country, I have successfully harvested

Backpacking is really about just getting there. So enjoy all the scenery along the way.

Weather out West can change quickly, so make sure you invest in quality gear.

numerous elk, bighorn sheep, mountain goat, Coues deer, and mule deer on public land.

I prefer to backpack in to get away from areas that are easily accessible. A current topographic map or one of the satellite imagery Web sites can really help show you where the more remote areas are located. My main focus is any area that is too far from roads or campgrounds to be accessed by day hunters. I also look for varying topography and cover with some obvious high points to use as scouting locations. When backpacking, my load usually weighs 45 to 50 pounds, which includes my bow. This is enough gear to support me comfortably for a five- or six-day hunt.

When searching for a pack to buy, pay attention to how many cubic inches of capacity is listed on the pack. I like a durable pack with plenty of space. If possible, go to a mountaineering or specialty camping or hunting store. They can help you choose a pack that will work for your needs. They can also instruct you on how to adjust the straps so that the pack fits you and carries properly. The majority of the weight should ride on your hips. Don't buy a cheap pack. As with most other things, in backpacks you get what you pay for.

When selecting a pack, be sure to get one that can support a lot of weight. Although there are some great internal frames on the market, I prefer to use an external-frame pack because I think it is easier to keep adding to your load if necessary. For example, awkward or heavy items such as meat, antlers, or horns can easily be strapped or tied onto the frame. The only limit is how much weight you can carry.

When planning, don't forget that in the Rockies fall temperatures can fluctuate from below freezing to boiling hot so you need to be prepared for heat, rain, snow, and wind. My standard gear for hunting the Rocky Mountains in late August or September at elevations of 7,000 to 10,000 feet includes the following:

SUGGESTED EQUIPMENT FOR A FIVE-DAY, FOUR-NIGHT TRIP

Clothes
1 wool balaclava full face/head covering
1 pair lightweight gloves
3 pair socks
2 pair long underwear
2 pair long underwear tops
1 pair camo pants
1 long-sleeve camo shirt
1 lightweight camo jacket with hood
1 camouflage headnet
1 set lightweight raingear

Food/Utensils
4 freeze-dried dinners (just add water)
4 packages ramen noodles
4 packages hot chocolate
10 packets of instant oatmeal
5 granola bars
5 Wilderness athlete energy bars
1/2 pound jerky
1 lightweight stove
1 fuel canister for stove
1 small pot
1 cup
1 fork
Matches and lighter

Equipment
Bow
6 arrows w/razor-sharp broadheads
Extra bowstring
Finger tab, glove, or release
GPS and topo map of the area
Digital camera
Knife with sharpening stone
Binoculars 10–32 (Zeiss)
Spotting scope 10–45 (Zeiss)
Tripod (lightweight fold-up)
2 water bottles
Water filtration system
Smoke in a bottle (wind detector)
Small flashlight w/extra batteries
Toilet paper
100-foot parachute cord
Sleeping bag
Dome tent (with rain fly)
Small, wind-up alarm clock
Toothbrush and toothpaste
No-scent deodorant
Small bottle of shampoo
1 hand towel
2 large mesh game bags
1 pound salt for cape or hide

* In remote areas, a satellite phone or small two-way radio is a great idea. Although they add weight, either could save your life in a bad situation.

Always carry emergency gear, such as a radio or satellite phone.

Make sure that water is readily available. In most Western states, find-ing a water source isn't too difficult. A preseason scouting trip can con-firm that you won't run dry while hunting. When backpacking by yourself or with others, always leave behind with someone a detailed map or the coordinates of where you will be and when you plan to return. Just this simple precaution could save your life.

Whenever possible, I try to scout any locations I am interested in before the season. I usually head to the highest point in the area I plan to hunt and let my optics do all the work. In my opinion, good optics are a must for this type of scouting or hunting. I prefer a variable-power spot-ting scope with a minimum of 45 power on the top end. I also suggest 8X or 10X for handheld optics. My two favorite optics manufacturers are Zeiss and Swarovski. You can scout a lot more country with good optics than you ever could by walking. Cheap optics often cause eyestrain and headaches. Although high-quality optics are expensive, they will help you be a more successful hunter. When hunting for mule deer, it is not uncom-mon to spend six to eight hours a day looking through binoculars or a spotting scope. So purchase the best optics you can afford. Furthermore, by scouting with optics, you get the additional benefit of not spooking the game or leaving scent everywhere.

I also research what is legal and try to have as many tags as possible for the game I could possibly harvest. It seems that every time I go after

Good optics are a must for scouting or hunting out West. Here I am glassing open country for bedded mule deer.

elk, I spot monster mule deer and bear, or vice versa. Having multiple tags just increases your odds of being successful and packing out some fresh meat.

When guiding or hunting for myself, I will glass until I find an animal that is in a position for me to stalk it. It is always best to wait until the animal is in a position to stalk before moving in and possibly blowing him out of the area. Sometimes it is difficult to do, but it's best to watch an animal for three days and stalk him once when conditions are perfect rather than trying to move in prematurely. Oftentimes, by watching an individual animal for days, you can learn his individual habits and favorite haunts.

The great thing about backpacking is that if the animals aren't in your area, you can pick up and change locations.

Two of my most memorable backpack hunts were both on public land in the mountains of Colorado. The first was an elk hunt 20 years ago in the Arapaho National Forest just west of Lost Lake. I talked a former girlfriend into going along, with promises of a relaxing four days of fishing for brook trout and camping out in the wilderness. I assured her I was just bringing my bow along in case we ran into any elk.

By the second day, I'd had all the relaxing and fishing I could stand. I took off for an evening hunt with bow in hand. I explained to the poor girl

You can use a backpack to hunt remote areas that often hold more abundant and less pressured game.

(who was scared of being alone) that I would be back by dark. Things never seem to work out as you plan, and this hunt was no exception. I had gone quite a ways that evening into a big valley with lots of drainages and dark timber. I won't say I was totally lost, but I was a little turned around. I decided to let out a few cow calls and if nothing happened, I figured I had better sort out how to get back to the tent before dark. I was just about to get up, assuming that nothing was within earshot of my calls, when two elk came into view. They were looking in my direction and one mewed softly while walking toward me. They were looking for the source of those cow calls in that downed timber.

As the lead cow came quartering past me, I let the string drop. Even at that angle, I felt the shot was too far back and a little high. They both bolted at the shot, and the dark timber swallowed them up in seconds. I was all alone and trying to figure out my next move. I waited 30 minutes before sneaking over in the near darkness. In my haste to leave camp and go hunting, I had left behind my flashlight and compass. (I was young— what can I say?) I spotted some blood right away, but it was getting too dark to follow the trail.

Unfortunately, it was also too dark for me to figure out how to get back to camp. I made an executive decision. It was warm, so I decided to spend the night right there on the blood trail. I figured I could hike out to camp the next morning right after I trailed my elk. Not long after dark, I was running in place trying to keep warm. It was a miserably cold night and one of the longest I have spent outdoors. When I could finally see, I took up the blood trail. My cow was lying dead only about 100 yards away. My arrow had been high and too far back, but luckily I had managed to hit the main artery just below the spine, and she had bled out quickly.

After blazing a few trees in the dark timber, I made it out to a place I recognized. I hurried back to camp to find a very agitated young woman with zero understanding about how cool it was that I had shot an elk. She swore that a bear had circled around the tent that night and that she could hear it breathing. I think she just made that part up to make me feel worse. There were a few bear tracks, but it was hard to say how old they were. Seven hours later, on our second trip back in to the elk to backpack out the remaining meat, she realized that our relationship probably wasn't going to work out. Of course, she didn't say it quite as nicely as that!

My other favorite backpack hunt was for mule deer with a good friend of mine. We headed deep into the mountains to set up camp. After a few days of unsuccessful glassing and hiking, we packed up and moved to a lower elevation. Almost immediately we started seeing more deer. I hiked down to a small meadow where we had glassed some deer moving in. I decided to set up behind a fallen tree in a small strip of aspens.

There is a certain feeling of freedom when you carry everything you need to live on your back.

I had been sitting for only about 10 minutes when I heard some thrashing to my left and spotted a 3 x 3 muley buck about 40 yards away working the velvet off his antlers. The small aspen he was using was whipping around him like a signal flag. When the buck finished with the aspen, he started walking slowly down the trail toward me. That is when I saw him. Not far behind the first buck was a monster 4 x 4 muley. He was the biggest buck I had ever seen, the type you see on magazine covers or painted on old Remington calendars. I just knew what was going to happen. I was going to let the smaller buck pass by me and then I was going to nail the big buck.

As they closed to about 30 yards, the small buck veered off the trail and started angling directly toward me. The big buck stayed on the trail and continued on his course, which would take him past me broadside at close to 15 yards. As the younger buck closed to about 20 yards, I began to worry. The small buck was angling straight on toward me, and I still didn't have a shot at the big boy yet. The smaller deer turned broadside, and I made a decision and took the shot. My arrow zipped through both lungs and the buck traveled only about 80 yards before dropping. Now every time I look at his rack displayed on my wall at home, I wonder whatever happened to that big one.

My reason for sharing these two stories is that sometimes I feel

Packing out a mule deer. Proper meat and trophy care is important to prevent spoilage.

hunters get too wrapped up in pursuing trophies. I harvested that young 3 x 3 mule deer 17 years ago. And even though I have harvested bucks more than twice his size, this is still one of my favorite trophies. A trophy doesn't have to be a big buck. It doesn't even have to be a buck. I think that as bowhunters, we always need to keep trophies in perspective.

CARE OF HARVESTED GAME

If you're planning a backpack hunt, be sure you are prepared to care for an animal if you harvest one. There are some simple steps to prevent spoilage of the meat and trophy. Cooling the meat down as quickly as possible is your first priority. I prefer to bone all the meat out. This helps the meat cool faster and makes it easier to carry. Use flyproof, breathable game bags to hang the meat in a shady, cool spot if possible. I like spots near creeks or low-lying areas when available. If the weather is hot, pack the meat out as soon as possible. If you're not sure how to properly bone out a carcass, visit a butcher shop or game processing shop and learn from a pro.

Trophy care is also important. If the weather is warm, or it is going to be a few days before you reach a freezer or taxidermist, it is important to cape or skin out your animal to avoid hair slippage. This includes turning the ears and splitting the lips on capes, and properly fleshing and drying the cape or skin. If you can't do it, learn how. There are some great books and videos that show how to properly cape and skin an animal for a mount or rug. Taxidermists are also usually more than happy to show a hunter how to properly care for trophies in the field.

Practice makes perfect, so cape out any animals you don't plan on mounting for practice before you head afield on a backpack hunt.

12
SHOT PLACEMENT

Two of the most important aspects of successful bowhunting are knowing when and where to shoot an animal. When to shoot is most commonly learned through trial and error. When I think back on the times I miscalculated when to shoot, I realize that oftentimes my mistakes were due to my failure to pick up on the animal's body language. By studying and learning animal behavior, you can speed up your learning curve. Unfortunately, learning when to shoot is not cut-and-dried. There is no perfect formula for every encounter. The fact that no two animals or situations are ever the same makes this a knowledge that must be sensed as much as learned. Fortunately, there are some things we can do to become more efficient predators.

One of the best is training yourself to pick up on clues in the animal's body posture. I try to constantly monitor the animal's state of awareness. Certain body parts and what they are doing offer the observant hunter tips on the animal's state of mind. For example, if the ears are relaxed, swatting bugs, or swiveling slowly, the animal is calm and not aware of your presence.

Watch for signals in the animal's body posture.

This is a great time to draw and shoot if the animal is in range and at a good shot angle.

The things we need to watch out for while trying to determine when to draw and shoot are signs that the animal is alert or nervous. Things to look for include ears that are erect and cupped, a tail that is stiff, erect, or flared, or a stiff body or stiff walk. Any of these may be indications that the animal is nervous. An animal that is alert or nervous is more likely to react at the sound of your shot, increasing the likelihood of a missed shot, or even worse, a wounded animal. By shooting only at animals that are relaxed or not overly nervous, we improve our odds of making a good shot.

A bad decision on when to shoot can easily turn what could be a successful outcome into just another close-call story. A prime example is a mistake I made on a mule deer hunt. I was slowly stalking up on a bedded buck. He was facing away from me, and the wind was in my face. As I closed to about 20 yards from the buck, I started to move too fast. I knew I could make the shot. I just needed to take one more step, and the buck's vitals would be clear of brush. In my excitement, I stepped on a small rock that made a soft grating sound beneath my boot. The deer didn't turn its head, but both his ears swiveled and were cupped in my direction. I tried to rush the shot, and in my haste to draw my bow, the upper limb made a small noise when it hit a branch. The buck bolted out of his bed and left me standing there with my fingers still curled around my semi-taut bowstring. The outcome would have been different had I paid more attention to the buck's body language and not tried to rush the shot.

In hindsight, the buck obviously heard the noise when my boot grated on the rock. That is why he swiveled his ears. He wasn't too spooked, or I feel he

A wrong decision on when to shoot can send an animal bolting off.

would have jumped up or turned his head to look as well. He was, however, on high alert. What I should have done was stand perfectly still and waited for the buck to calm back down. Instead, in my excitement I tried to rush a shot at an already alert buck. When he heard my second mistake, the branch on my limb, he bolted. I obviously did not do a good job of choosing when to shoot.

By analyzing our mistakes and talking with other bowhunters, we can learn more about animals and their reactions. This can help us decide when to shoot on future hunts.

Even on small game such as wild turkeys, proper shot placement is critical. Here, my wife Michele is smiling with her first bow-killed turkey.

Sometimes all it takes to be successful is a general knowledge of the species you are after. A recent unsuccessful hunt for one of my non-guided clients could have been successful had he known more about elk. My client was an experienced whitetail hunter from south Texas, where he was familiar with the ultra-spooky traits of those hard-hunted deer. This was his first elk hunt, and we showed him some tree stands and ground blinds we had set up.

While talking with him at the end of his hunt, I learned that he had several close calls. He explained that at one point he had some elk directly below him while he was in one of our tree stands, but he was afraid to draw for fear of spooking them. He said they wandered off as quickly as they had shown up, and he never drew his bow. Since elk are not accustomed to being hunted from tree stands and are not nearly as spooky as whitetails, it is more than likely that he could have drawn and shot his elk at less than 10 yards. As it was, it sounded as though he was being overly cautious for the animal he was after.

Sometimes when to shoot has to be decided in a split second. An animal may turn its head, change directions, or do any number of other things that cause your window of opportunity to be brief. To prepare for a quick shot, I practice drawing fast and smooth. I also work on shooting quickly and accurately. I do most of my bowhunting with a recurve bow. I use this because the range at which I usually shoot most of my animals falls between 10 and 25 yards. At this distance, I can draw and shoot my bow in two seconds. When I shoot my compound, I also practice drawing quickly, acquiring my sight pin, and shooting. It doesn't matter what your bow of choice is. The key is becoming as quick and efficient with your weapon as possible. For increasing your opportunities in the field, practice shooting at different angles and from different positions. Also practice with the clothes you plan to wear while hunting, including gloves and head net if you plan to wear them.

Years ago, I learned the hard way to practice shooting with my gear ahead of time. I was wearing a baggy head net and was shooting with my fingers. My anchor point was to tuck the string tightly into the corner of my mouth. When a doe showed up on the trail I was sitting next to, I slowly drew my bow to full draw, tucked into my anchor, and released. At the shot, an unseen force thrust my face forward. It scared the hell out of me and it took me a minute to figure out what had happened. I finally realized that the metal nock on my string must have hung up

Avoid shots at animals that are nervous or looking at you.

on the loose mesh of my head net. So when I let the string go, it snatched the head net forward, throwing the arrow down into the ground, leaving me and one startled doe a little wiser for the experience.

When considering when to shoot, you have to take a lot of factors into account, and usually all at once. For example, when an animal is moving it is harder for it to spot movement. This can be a better time to draw than when an animal is stopped. Wind can cause trees, bushes, or grass to move, which can also help conceal your movement. When you're in the shadows, you are harder to spot than when you are in the sunlight. Sometimes an animal will make noise that you can use to cover your own noise, for example, a deer walking in dry leaves or an elk raking a tree. By taking advantage of one or all of these, you can increase your odds of being successful. So stay alert and be ready to take advantage of any opportunity you are presented with.

The other part of when to shoot is the animal's position in relationship to where you are. Before drawing, I check to make sure there is not another animal behind the one I am concentrating on. Never attempt a shot if there is any possibility the arrow may pass through your intended target and strike another animal.

In all situations, especially in suburban areas or small woodlots, it is also extremely important to make sure that you are shooting in a safe direction, where your arrow won't skip or deflect, endangering people or property.

If all is clear and you are ready to draw, the next decision is your most important: where to shoot. The highest-percentage shot on big game is an animal that is broadside or quartering away from you. It is important for bowhunters to realize why these are the best shots to take and where to aim on the animal to ensure a quick, clean kill. A broadhead kills by hemorrhaging. To work effectively, it needs to be placed where it can do the most damage to the most vital organs. Thanks to the National Bowhunter Education Foundation (NBEF), I have been given permission to include these diagrams to illustrate the correct location of the bone structure, organs, and circulatory systems for most of the animals I have discussed in this book. These diagrams are great for understanding where you need to place your arrow to ensure a quick, clean kill. They also show where other vital areas are in case you miss your mark.

There are many locations on an animal that, when struck by a strong, razor-sharp broadhead, will cause a quick, clean kill. They include the lungs, brain, the forward part of the spinal cord, the heart, and major arteries such as the femoral and carotid. The best possible shot, with the largest margin for error, is the lungs.

It is our responsibility to know where to shoot. It is also our responsibility to take only shots that are within our effective range. To hit

A quick, clean kill is every bowhunter's objective.

the center of the lungs on a broadside animal, pick a spot just below the centerline of the animal just forward of the crease of the shoulder. By aiming here, even if you are a little off, your arrow will still strike the lungs or other vital areas surrounding the lungs including the heart, liver, or spinal cord.

Although there are other areas on big game animals that will cause a quick kill, the margin for error is small and therefore these make difficult targets, especially considering it is tough to know the exact location since the vitals lie beneath hair and flesh. Most misses or nonfatal shots are caused when a bowhunter tries to force a shot or tries to shoot at an animal beyond his or her effective range.

If you are not confident of a good hit, it is always best to pass up the shot. I have passed up many low-percentage shots, only to be pleasantly surprised when the animal moved closer or I was able to sneak closer for a perfect opportunity.

If you can't take a broadside shot, a quartering-away shot can be just as deadly. With the knowledge of where the lungs are located, it is easy to see on the chart how you can aim farther back on a quartering-away animal so that your arrow strikes the rear half of the lung on your side and the forward half of the lung on the opposite side. If the animal is

Animals that are quartering toward you offer only low-percentage shots.

quartering hard enough that you cannot see the last few ribs in front of the abdomen, it is best not to shoot.

When hunting from a tree stand or shooting at an animal at a steep uphill or downhill angle, you will have to adjust your shot accordingly. For shooting at an animal uphill, your point of aim will have to be lower

If you don't have a good shot, it is always best to pass up the shot or wait for a better angle.

to strike both lungs. When shooting at an animal downhill or from a tree stand, you will have to adjust your aiming point a little higher. If the animal is at too steep an angle above or below you, it is best not to shoot, because it is possible to hit only one lung and lose the animal.

I've gotten into the habit of performing a necropsy on every animal I harvest with a bow. I also check out clients' and friends' kills whenever possible. It is interesting to note exactly where the arrow struck and how quickly the animal went down. Knowledge of the animal you are after and where its vitals are located can be your most valuable asset when bowhunting.

As bowhunters, we all continue on our own path of learning as we go. The failures we encounter are experiences that just make it that much sweeter when everything comes together as it did in our dreams the night before. Introduce everyone you can to our great outdoor sport. And don't forget to take the time to enjoy every sunrise, sunset, and everything in between.

You must change your aiming point when shooting at an uphill or downhill angle.

13

FOLLOW-UP AFTER THE SHOT

THIS SECTION APPLIES TO ALL ARROW-SHOT ANIMALS OF ANY SPECIES.

I t is a fact that if you hunt long enough and shoot at enough animals, you will make some less-than-perfect shots. All the true bowhunters I know respect and admire the animals they pursue. They know their equipment, they know their limitations, and they take only ethical shots. Even with precautions, mistakes do happen. I have included this section on follow-up after the shot because I feel that it will help many bowhunters make the best decisions after their shots. I feel qualified to write this because I have trailed hundreds of bow-shot big game animals all over the United States, Canada, and Africa. I have learned from every animal I have harvested with a bow as well as from trailing hundreds of my clients' animals. If this chapter helps even one fellow bowhunter recover an animal that would have otherwise been lost, then it will have been worth the time and effort that I put into writing it.

It all happened so fast. You released the arrow. Your animal went crashing off into the brush. What do you do now? First, try to assess your shot. With luck, you were able to see the arrow impact and have a feel for where it hit and what type of penetration you got. Bear in mind that sometimes what you think happened and what actually happened are two different things.

One great clue as to what and where your arrow hit is the noise it made. If you heard a loud crack, odds are your arrow struck a heavy bone, such as the shoulder, front or hind legs, vertebrae, or hip. Very little noise, a soft thump, or a dull crack usually means a paunch shot, a glancing blow, or a neck or ham hit. A nice, solid thump usually means right in the chest. It takes practice and is certainly not foolproof, but if you really pay attention to the noise your arrow makes when it strikes, it can give you clues as to where your arrow hit the animal. Your arrow can also give you valuable clues about how to proceed after the shot. Bright, frothy blood is common when you make a lung shot. An arrow that smells strongly or has greenish-brown matter on it means the arrow passed through the stomach or intestines. Arrows that feel greasy or that have pieces of fat on the shaft

You can often figure out where your arrow struck the animal by studying cut hair and its color.

or the broadhead usually mean a shot that was too high, too low, or through the edge of one of the hind legs or hams. An arrow that is covered in dark red blood may mean a liver or kidney shot.

Other clues include hair found at the point of impact. This is where you need to know the animal you are hunting. Study photographs and video of the species you are after. Hair and its different length or color can help you figure out where your arrow entered the animal. Note that I said entered the animal. Remember that the majority of the cut hair you will find will be where the arrow entered, not where it exited.

Always carry some type of trail marking system with you. I prefer toilet paper, since it is biodegradable. If it is windy, snowing, raining, or if there is a chance you will need to return the next day, I prefer bright red or orange surveyor's tape. Just be sure to pick this up when you're done. By marking the animal's blood trail or tracks every few yards, you can get a sense of the animal's direction of travel, which can help you find the next track or spot of blood.

As I mentioned earlier, sometimes what we think we saw is far from what actually took place. I blame this partly on our own minds wanting desperately to see a solid hit. I once had a client who, after shooting about a foot over a bull's chest, jumped up and down and exclaimed that he "nailed" him. He saw the arrow flying above the bull and swore that he had a pass-through. He was so adamant that I started to doubt what I had seen. It was only after we finally found the bloodless arrow that he believed my account of what happened.

Another time, while in Texas with outfitter Mike Palmer, one of his clients came in and said he had double-lunged a big whitetail. He explained that it was broadside and he was sure it was a perfect hit. He said he had tried to trail it but lost the blood trail. We went out with him and when we did finally find the buck, the arrow was in the buck's hindquarter. Mike's client actually said: "That can't be my arrow." In his mind, the shot had been perfect.

I have been guilty of similar cases of mistaken arrow placement. If you shoot enough animals, odds are if it hasn't already happened to you, it will. Oftentimes mistakenly calling where the arrow hit is a result of the animal's reaction to the shot. Some animals are actually ducking, spinning, moving, or all three when the arrow strikes. This tends to happen more when an animal is alert, nervous, or looking at you. Shots at animals that display one or more of the above characteristics are lower-percentage shots.

Besides the sound of the hit and looking at the arrow, watching an animal's reaction to the shot will give you clues about shot placement.

If the animal runs only a short distance and stops and starts walking slowly with its head down, it is probably a stomach or intestine shot.

Alert or nervous animals can react quickly to the sound of your bow.

Sometimes paunch-shot animals (animals shot in the stomach or intestines) won't run at all, but will walk slowly away, head down and tail twitching—both usually are indications of a paunch hit. Animals hit in the paunch generally bed down close by. If you have struck an animal in the paunch, a good rule of thumb is to memorize where you last saw the animal and slowly and quietly leave the area. I prefer to wait at least 10 hours when possible before trailing. Paunch-shot animals rarely travel uphill and will often head toward water. Blood trails are usually minimal, and oftentimes you will find drops of fluid or pieces of stomach or intestinal matter.

Sometimes a shot behind the lungs will result in a liver or kidney shot. The animal usually reacts the same way as a paunch-hit animal, but the blood trail will usually be easier to follow. Animals that have been shot in the liver or kidney tend to die much quicker than those shot in the stomach or intestines.

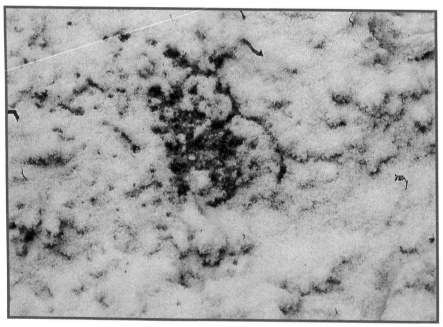

Study what you see. Here the deer we were trailing stopped in the snow to watch its back trail. The grazed deer was fine, but we followed him up as far as possible just to be sure.

Animals that are shot in the brisket, struck with a glancing blow, or shot in a nonvital area in the body usually bolt off, running a short distance. They tend to bleed a lot for the first hundred yards or so. Then the blood trail usually tapers off. These animals are usually not fatally hit and are rarely recovered unless another shot can be made. I prefer to trail these hits almost immediately in hopes of another shot opportunity.

Arrows that strike the leg/scapula joint (shoulder) rarely penetrate much past the broadhead. These animals usually bolt off, leaving a relatively sparse blood trail, and generally recover from the wound. Again, I prefer to trail these animals immediately as well, in hopes of getting another shot.

Shots that strike the ham usually cause the animal to jump and run a short distance, then walk slowly before bedding down. These shots are usually fatal, because there are a lot of veins and arteries running through the hindquarters. These hits usually bleed well and are easy to trail. I usually wait two to three hours before following the animal. Sometimes such a hit requires a follow-up shot on an animal that is incapacitated.

Arrows that strike the neck are fatal if they sever the spinal cord or cause enough damage to either major arteries or the windpipe. Hits like these are usually instantly incapacitating in the case of the spinal cord or usually within 100 yards in the case of a severed artery or windpipe. The blood trail is usually easy to follow. Other neck shots are superficial and although they may bleed profusely at first, the blood trail will peter out soon afterwards. Neck-hit animals tend to run hard, especially if the arrow is still in the animal. I usually follow these shots up after only about 15 minutes.

Head shots are usually fatal only if the brain is hit. If you shoot an animal in the head or jaw and it runs off, give the animal 30 minutes and

When trailing, sometimes the blood trail is obvious.

very slowly take up the trail. Blood is usually easy to follow, but a follow-up shot is the best you can usually hope for.

If the arrow has broken a leg or cut major arteries in the leg, the animal can oftentimes be recovered. I believe in pushing most extremity hits to keep the animals from bedding up and stopping the flow of blood. For leg hits, whether the arrow breaks the leg or not, I slowly but steadily stay on the trail. As with any blood trail, I try to go as quietly as possible, because with a leg hit a follow-up shot is usually required. Don't worry if you keep jumping the animal, as that is usually your only hope of recovery.

At other times, a blood trail is not so easy to notice.

Unfortunately, some animals that are hit will never be recovered. I am confident that most animals not found recover fully.

If your arrow hits the chest cavity and makes that solid "whump" sound, you will probably see or hear the animal go down. A solid double-lung or heart shot will usually take down the biggest animals in North America in seconds. Even if you feel your shot is perfect, just to be safe, it is best to wait 30 minutes before trailing. A heart- or lung-shot animal usually runs until it expires a short distance away. A central to lower lung hit or heart shot usually leaves a very obvious blood trail. High double-lung shots, especially those without an exit hole, are usually harder to trail even though the animal will usually not go more than 100 yards. In situations where poor penetration or a bad angle causes only one lung to be hit, your odds of recovery are severely reduced. In situations where I feel I may have hit only one lung, I wait 30 minutes and then trail the animal. They usually bed up shortly after being hit, but generally a second arrow is needed to anchor the animal. In a lot of cases, the animal fully recovers from a single-lung or partial-lung hit.

A prime example of this happened a few years ago when the late Rob Pedretti, my friend and business partner at the time, was kicked by our burro in a cross-country burro race in Colorado. Rob knew he was hurt, but continued to run 3 miles to finish the race. He had blood in his mouth and was rushed to a hospital and fully recovered. The burro had cracked one of his ribs, which then punctured one of his lungs, much as a broadhead would have done. He was still able to run 3 miles in that condition. Rob was in incredible shape, and animals are much tougher than humans, so it is common for them to recover from what we think would be a fatal shot.

If the animal falls instantly to the ground after being shot, odds are

For the competent bowhunter who chooses his or her shots wisely, quick, clean kills are the norm.

that you partially severed, or shocked the spinal cord by hitting the vertebrae. In this situation, even if the animal seems to be down and out . . . shoot again. Spine shots are tricky business, and I have seen animals that dropped like a stone get up and take off seconds later when they were only temporarily paralyzed. Sometimes they just lose function in their hind legs (partial paralysis) and sometimes the spinal cord is severed, which leads to a quick death. In my opinion, you should always put a follow-up shot into any animal when given the opportunity, especially a spine-shot animal.

Practice will help you make the shot when it counts.

In my experience, with the exception of a gut shot, your arrow either causes enough hemorrhaging to kill the animal or the animal eventually recovers. I know of many occasions where animals were shot and not recovered, only to be seen again months later, apparently well and healthy. They had recovered fully from their nonfatal wounds. This is another reason to use only razor-sharp broadheads. They either kill the animal or the clean cut heals up quickly. Out of respect for the animals we pursue, large or small, I feel it is every bowhunter's responsibility to pursue all wounded animals to the best of their ability.

DIFFICULT TRAILS

When blood trails are hard to find due to weather conditions, arrow placement, or when trailing long-haired animals, follow these guidelines and take special care when searching for sign. Go slowly, on your hands and knees if necessary, to stay on track. If tracks aren't obvious, look for scuff marks, hair, broken grass, twigs, or anything out of place. Be sure to check trees or bushes for blood as well. The blood and how high or low it is found can give you clues about where your arrow struck. Blood on two sides of the animal's tracks usually means a pass-through. If the trail can't be found, grid searches of the area are your best bet.

Take special care when trailing a wounded bear or mountain lion. Although attacks on humans are extremely rare, even when bears or lions are wounded, it can happen.

There is a great deal of satisfaction that comes with cleanly harvesting any animal.

Appendix A

P&Y Score Sheets for

Elk
Mule Deer
Black Bear
Antelope
Whitetail
Mt. Lion/Cougar

POPE & YOUNG CLUB

Official Scoring System for Bowhunting North American Big Game

MINIMUM SCORE
260

TYPICAL
YELLOWSTONE ELK (AMERICAN)

☐ IN VELVET

Detail of Point Measurement

Abnormal Points	
Right Antler	Left Antler
SUBTOTALS	
TOTAL TO E	

SEE OTHER SIDE FOR INSTRUCTIONS

				COLUMN 1	COLUMN 2	COLUMN 3	COLUMN 4
A. No. Points on Right Antler		No. Points on Left Antler		Spread Credit	Right Antler	Left Antler	Difference
B. Tip to Tip Spread		C. Greatest Spread					
D. Inside Spread of Main Beams		SPREAD CREDIT MAY EQUAL BUT NOT EXCEED LONGER MAIN BEAM					
E. Total of Lengths of Abnormal Points							
F. Length of Main Beam							
G-1. Length of First Point							
G-2. Length of Second Point							
G-3. Length of Third Point							
G-4. Length of Fourth Point							
G-5. Length of Fifth Point							
G-6. Length of Sixth Point, If Present							
G-7. Length of Seventh Point, If Present							
H-1. Circumference at Smallest Place Between First and Second Points							
H-2. Circumference at Smallest Place Between Second and Third Points							
H-3. Circumference at Smallest Place Between Third and Fourth Points							
H-4. Circumference at Smallest Place Between Fourth and Fifth Points							
		TOTALS					

ADD	Column 1		Location of Kill:	(County)	(State/Prov)
	Column 2		Date Killed:	Hunter:	
	Column 3		Owner:	Telephone #: ( )	
	Subtotal		Owner's Address:		
SUBTRACT Column 4			Guide's Name and Address:		
FINAL SCORE			Remarks: (Mention Any Abnormalities or Unique Qualities)		

Here are is a score sheet for typical elk. The instructions are on the following page.

I, _____ , certify that I have measured this trophy on _____
_{PRINT NAME} MM/DD/YYYYY

at _____
STREET ADDRESS   CITY   STATE/PROVINCE   ZIP CODE

and that these measurements and data are, to the best of my knowledge and belief, made in accordance with the instructions given.

Witness: _____ Signature: _____
TO MEASURER'S SIGNATURE   P&Y OFFICIAL MEASURER

_____
ADDRESS

_____
CITY   STATE/PROVINCE   ZIP

BRIEF INSTRUCTIONS FOR MEASURING TYPICAL YELLOWSTONE (AMERICAN) ELK

Measurements must be made with a flexible steel tape or steel cable and recorded to the nearest one-eighth of an inch. To simplify addition, please enter fractional figures in eighths and in proper fractions. Refer to **P & Y Measurer's Manual** for a detailed description of measuring procedures.

A. Number of Points on each antler. To be counted a point, a projection must be at least one inch long AND, at some location at least one inch from the tip, the length of the projection must exceed its width. Beam tip is counted as a point but not measured as a point.

B. Tip to Tip Spread is measured between tips of main beams.

C. Greatest Spread is measured between perpendiculars at a right angle to the center line of the skull at widest part whether across main beams or points.

D. Inside Spread of Main Beam is measured at a right angle to the center line of the skull at widest point between main beams. Enter this measurement again in "Spread Credit" column if it is less than or equal to the length of longer main beam. If greater, enter longer main beam length for Spread Credit.

E. Total of Length of Abnormal Points. Abnormal points are generally considered to be those non-typical in location (such as points originating from a point or from bottom or sides of main beam), or pattern (extra points, not generally paired). Sketch all abnormal points on antler illustration (front of form) showing location and length. Measure in usual manner and enter in appropriate blanks.

F. Length of Main Beam is measured from the center of the lowest outside edge of burr over outer curve to the most distant point of the main beam. Begin measuring at the location on the burr where the center line along the outer curve of the beam intersects the burr.

G-1-2-3-4-5-6-7. Length of Normal Points. Normal points project from the top of the main beam as shown in illustration. They are measured from the top edge of the main beam (baseline), over their outer curve, to their tip. To establish the appropriate baseline, lay a tape or (preferably) a cable on the top edge of the beam on each side of the point and draw a line under the cable to reflect the top edge of the beam, as if the point was not present. Record point lengths in appropriate blanks.

H-1-2-3-4. Circumferences. Circumferences are taken at the smallest place between corresponding normal points, as illustrated. If G-5 is missing, take H-4 halfway between the center of G-4 and beam tip. Circumference measurements must be taken with a steel tape (a cable cannot be used for these measurements).

ENTRY REQUIREMENTS

1. **Original scoring form** completed by an Official Measurer of the Pope & Young Club or the Boone & Crockett Club.
2. **Completed Fair Chase Affidavit.**
3. **Three photos of antlers, horns, or skull** (a view from the front side, a view from the left side and a view from the right side). A field photo is also requested, if possible.
4. **25.00 recording fee** (made payable to the Pope and Young Club)

Drying Period: To be eligible for entry in the Pope & Young Records, a trophy must first have been stored under normal room temperature and humidity for at least 60 days after date of kill. No trophy will be considered which has been altered in any way from its natural state.

POPE & YOUNG CLUB

Official Scoring System for Bowhunting North American Big Game

MINIMUM SCORE
mule deer	145
Columbian blacktail	90
Sitka blacktail	75

TYPICAL
MULE DEER AND BLACKTAIL DEER

KIND OF DEER (check one)
- ☐ mule deer
- ☐ Columbian blacktail
- ☐ Sitka blacktail
- ☐ **IN VELVET**

Detail of Point Measurement

Abnormal Points	
Right Antler	Left Antler

SUBTOTALS	
TOTAL TO E	

SEE OTHER SIDE FOR INSTRUCTIONS				COLUMN 1	COLUMN 2	COLUMN 3	COLUMN 4
				Spread Credit	Right Antler	Left Antler	Difference
A. No. Points on Right Antler		No. Points on Left Antler					
B. Tip to Tip Spread		C. Greatest Spread					
D. Inside Spread of Main Beams		SPREAD CREDIT MAY EQUAL BUT NOT EXCEED LONGER MAIN BEAM					
E. Total of Lengths of Abnormal Points							
F. Length of Main Beam							
G-1. Length of First Point, If Present							
G-2. Length of Second Point							
G-3. Length of Third Point, If Present							
G-4. Length of Fourth Point, If Present							
H-1. Circumference at Smallest Place Between Burr and First Point							
H-2. Circumference at Smallest Place Between First and Second Points							
H-3. Circumference at Smallest Place Between Main Beam and Third Point							
H-4. Circumference at Smallest Place Between Second and Fourth Points							
			TOTALS				

ADD	Column 1		Location of Kill:	(County)	(State/Prov)
	Column 2		Date Killed:	Hunter:	
	Column 3		Owner:	Telephone #: ( )	
	Subtotal		Owner's Address:		
SUBTRACT Column 4			Guide's Name and Address:		
FINAL SCORE			Remarks: (Mention Any Abnormalities or Unique Qualities)		

Here are is a score sheet for typical mule deer. The instructions are on the following page.

I, _____ , certify that I have measured this trophy on _____
PRINT NAME MM/DD/YYYY

at _____
STREET ADDRESS   CITY   STATE/PROVINCE   ZIP CODE

and that these measurements and data are, to the best of my knowledge and belief, made in accordance with the instructions given.

Witness: _____ Signature: _____
TO MEASURER'S SIGNATURE   P&Y OFFICIAL MEASURER

_____
ADDRESS

_____
CITY   STATE/PROVINCE   ZIP

BRIEF INSTRUCTIONS FOR MEASURING TYPICAL MULE AND BLACKTAIL DEER

Measurements must be made with a flexible steel tape or steel cable and recorded to the nearest one-eighth of an inch. To simplify addition, please enter fractional figures in eighths and in proper fractions. Refer to **P & Y Measurer's Manual** for a detailed description of measuring procedures.

A. Number of Points on each antler. To be counted a point, a projection must be at least one inch long AND, at some location at least one inch from the tip, the length of the projection must exceed its width. Beam tip is counted as a point but not measured as a point.

B. Tip to Tip Spread is measured between tips of main beams.

C. Greatest Spread is measured between perpendiculars at a right angle to the center line of the skull at widest part whether across main beams or points.

D. Inside Spread of Main Beam is measured at a right angle to the center line of the skull at widest point between main beams. Enter this measurement again in "Spread Credit" column if it is less than or equal to the length of longer main beam. If greater, enter longer main beam length for Spread Credit.

E. Total of Length of Abnormal Points. Abnormal points are generally considered to be those non-typical in location (such as points originating from a point or from bottom or sides of main beam). Sketch all abnormal points on antler illustration (front of form) showing location and length. Measure in usual manner and enter in appropriate blanks.

F. Length of Main Beam is measured from the center of the lowest outside edge of burr over outer curve to the most distant point of the main beam. Begin measuring at the location on the burr where the center line along the outer curve of the beam intersects the burr.

G-1-2-3-4. Length of Normal Points. Normal points are the brow points and the upper and lower forks as shown in illustration. They are measured from top edge of beam (baseline), over outer curve, to tip: with the exception of the G-3, which is measured from a baseline established along the edge of the G-2 point. To establish the appropriate baseline, lay a tape or (preferably) a cable on the top edge of the beam on each side of the point and draw a line under the cable to reflect the top edge of the beam as if the point was not present. Record point lengths in appropriate blanks.

H-1-2-3-4. Circumferences. Circumferences are taken at the smallest place between corresponding normal points, as illustrated. If first point is missing, take H-1 and H-2 at smallest place between burr and second point. If third point is missing, take H-3 halfway between the base and tip of the second point. If the fourth point is missing, take H-4 halfway between the center of the baseline for the second point and tip of main beam. Circumference measurements must be taken with a steel tape (a cable cannot be used for these measurements).

ENTRY REQUIREMENTS

1. **Original scoring form** completed by an Official Measurer of the Pope & Young Club or the Boone & Crockett Club.
2. **Completed Fair Chase Affidavit.**
3. **Three photos of antlers, horns, or skull** (a view from the front side, a view from the left side and a view from the right side). A field photo is also requested, if possible.
4. **$25.00 recording fee** (made payable to the Pope and Young Club)

Drying Period: To be eligible for entry in the Pope & Young Records, a trophy must first have been stored under normal room temperature and humidity for at least 60 days after date of kill. No trophy will be considered which has been altered in any way from its natural state.

POPE & YOUNG CLUB

Official Scoring System for Bowhunting North American Big Game

MINIMUM SCORE		BEAR	SEX	KIND OF BEAR (check one)
black bear	18		☐ Male	☐ black bear
grizzly bear	19		☐ Female	☐ grizzly
Alaska brown bear	20			☐ Alaska brown bear
polar bear	20			☐ polar

SEE OTHER SIDE FOR INSTRUCTIONS		MEASUREMENTS
A. Greatest Length Without Lower Jaw	(Measured in Sixteenths)	
B. Greatest Width	(Measured in Sixteenths)	
	FINAL SCORE	

Location of Kill: _____ (County) _____ (State/Prov)

Date Killed: _____ Hunter: _____

Owner: _____ Telephone #: ( )

Owner's Address: _____

Guide's Name and Address: _____

Were dogs used in conjunction with the pursuit and harvest of this animal? ☐ YES ☐ NO

If yes, the following statements apply:

1. I was present at the time that the dogs were initially released to pursue this animal.
2. If electronic collars were attached to any of the dogs, at no time from the beginning of the chase until the harvest of this animal were receivers used in the pursuit and harvest.

To the best of my knowledge the above statements are true. If #1 & #2 do not apply, please explain on a seperate sheet.

_____ _____
HUNTER'S SIGNATURE   MM/DD/YYYYY

I, _____ , certify that I have measured this trophy on _____
PRINT NAME   MM/DD/YYYYY

at _____
STREET ADDRESS   CITY   STATE/PROVINCE   ZIP CODE

and that these measurements and data are, to the best of my knowledge and belief, made in accordance with the instructions given.

Witness: _____ Signature: _____
TO MEASURER'S SIGNATURE   P&Y OFFICIAL MEASURER

_____
ADDRESS

_____
CITY   STATE/PROVINCE   ZIP

Here are is a score sheet for bear. The instructions are on the following page.

BRIEF INSTRUCTIONS FOR MEASURING BEAR

Measurements must be made with a flexible steel tape and recorded to the nearest one-sixteenth of an inch. Calipers or a skull box may be used. To simplify addition, please enter fractional figures in sixteenths and in proper fractions. Refer to **P & Y Measurer's Manual** for a detailed description of measuring procedures.

A. Greatest Length is measured between perpendiculars to the long axis of the skull WITHOUT the lower jaw, and EXCLUDING malformations. (Normal teeth are included)

B. Greatest Width is measured between perpendiculars at right angles to the long axis.

All adhering flesh, membrane, and cartilage MUST be completely removed before the drying period begins and official measurements are taken.

IF DOGS ARE USED, THE HUNTER MUST BE PRESENT AT THE TIME THE DOGS ARE RELEASED AND NO ELECTRONIC COLLARS CAN BE USED IN THE PURSUIT

ENTRY REQUIREMENTS

1. **Original scoring form** completed by an Official Measurer of the Pope & Young Club or the Boone & Crockett Club.
2. **Completed Fair Chase Affidavit.**
3. **Three photos of antlers, horns, or skull** (a view from the front side, a view from the left side and a view from the right side). A field photo is also requested, if possible. The front view is best taken from above at a 45-degree angle.
4. **$25.00 recording fee** (made payable to the Pope and Young Club)

Drying Period: To be eligible for entry in the Pope & Young Records, a trophy must first have been stored under normal room temperature and humidity for at least 60 days after date of kill. No trophy will be considered which has been altered in any way from its natural state.

All flesh and membrane MUST be removed from skull prior to the drying period.

POPE & YOUNG CLUB

Official Scoring System for Bowhunting North American Big Game

MINIMUM SCORE
67

PRONGHORN ANTELOPE

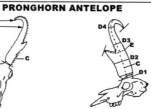

SEE OTHER SIDE FOR INSTRUCTIONS		COLUMN 1	COLUMN 2	COLUMN 3
A. Tip to Tip Spread		Right Horn	Left Horn	Difference
B. Inside Spread				
C. Length of Horn				
D-1. Circumference of Base				
D-2. Circumference at First Quarter (taken BELOW prong) (This measurement taken at ___ inches from base)				
D-3. Circumference at Second Quarter (taken ABOVE prong) (This measurement taken at ___ inches from base)				
D-4. Circumference at Third Quarter (This measurement taken at ___ inches from base)				
E. Length of Prong				
TOTALS				

ADD	Column 1		Location of Kill:	(County)	(State/Prov)
	Column 2		Date Killed:	Hunter:	
	Subtotal		Owner:	Telephone #: ( )	
SUBTRACT Column 3			Owner's Address:		
FINAL SCORE			Guide's Name and Address:		
			Remarks: (Mention Any Abnormalities or Unique Qualities)		

At the time of official measurement, were the sheaths reattched to the cores by the use of some type of filler or adhesive? ☐ YES ☐ NO

(If "yes," the D-1 value can not exceed the D-2 value on the same horn. If so, enter the actual D-1 measurement in the remarks section and record the D-2 measurement as the D-1 value in its respective column.)

I, _____ , certify that I have measured this trophy on _____
PRINT NAME   MM/DD/YYYYY

at _____
STREET ADDRESS   CITY   STATE/PROVINCE   ZIP CODE

and that these measurements and data are, to the best of my knowledge and belief, made in accordance with the instructions given.

Witness: _____ Signature: _____
TO MEASURER'S SIGNATURE   P&Y OFFICIAL MEASURER

_____
ADDRESS

_____
CITY   STATE/PROVINCE   ZIP

Here are is a score sheet for pronghorn antelope. The instructions are on the following page.

BRIEF INSTRUCTIONS FOR MEASURING PRONGHORN ANTELOPE

Measurements must be made with a flexible steel tape and recorded to the nearest one-eighth of an inch. To simplify addition, please enter fractional figures in eighths and in proper fractions. Refer to **P & Y Measurer's Manual** for a detailed description of measuring procedures.

A. Tip to Tip Spread measured between tip of horns.

B. Inside Spread of Horns measured at right angles to the center line of the skull at widest point between horns.

C. Length of Horn is measured on the outside curve, as illustrated. The line taken will vary with different heads, depending on the direction of the curvature. Measure along the center of the outer curve, from tip of horn, to a point in line with the lowest edge of the base, using a straight edge to establish the line end.

D-1.Circumference of Base is measured at right angles to long axis of the horn. Do not follow irregular edge of horn. The line of measurement must be entirely on horn material.

D-2-3-4 Circumferences. Divide measurement of longer horn by four. **Measuring from the base,** mark **BOTH** horns at these quarters even though one horn is shorter, and measure circumferences at these marks. Should D-2 land on the swelling of the prong, take D-2 measurement **immediately below** swelling of prong. Note D-3 **must** be taken above the prong. If D-3 falls on or below the prong, then take this measurement immediately **above** the prong. If adjustments for swelling of prong are made to the D-2 or D-3 measurement, note these adjustments in "REMARKS" section.

E. Length of Prong. Measure from the tip of the prong, **along the upper edge** of the outer side to the horn; then, around the horn, to a point at the rear of the horn where a straight edge across the back of both horns touches the horn. This measurement around the horn, from the base of the prong, should be taken at right angles to the long axis of the horn.

ENTRY REQUIREMENTS

1. **Original scoring form** completed by an Official Measurer of the Pope & Young Club or the Boone & Crockett Club.
2. **Completed Fair Chase Affidavit.**
3. **Three photos of antlers, horns, or skull** (a view from the front side, a view from the left side and a view from the right side). A field photo is also requested, if possible.
4. **$25.00 recording fee** (made payable to the Pope and Young Club)

Drying Period: To be eligible for entry in the Pope & Young Records, a trophy must first have been stored under normal room temperature and humidity for at least 60 days after date of kill. No trophy will be considered which has been altered in any way from its natural state.

POPE & YOUNG CLUB

Official Scoring System for Bowhunting North American Big Game

MINIMUM SCORE
whitetail 125
Coues' 65

TYPICAL
WHITETAIL AND COUES' DEER

KIND OF DEER (check one)
☐ whitetail
☐ Coues'

☐ IN VELVET

	Abnormal Points	
	Right Antler	Left Antler
SUBTOTALS		
TOTAL TO E		

SEE OTHER SIDE FOR INSTRUCTIONS		COLUMN 1	COLUMN 2	COLUMN 3	COLUMN 4
A. No. Points on Right Antler	No. Points on Left Antler	Spread Credit	Right Antler	Left Antler	Difference
B. Tip to Tip Spread	C. Greatest Spread				
D. Inside Spread of Main Beams	SPREAD CREDIT MAY EQUAL BUT NOT EXCEED LONGER MAIN BEAM				
E. Total of Lengths of Abnormal Points					
F. Length of Main Beam					
G-1. Length of First Point					
G-2. Length of Second Point					
G-3. Length of Third Point					
G-4. Length of Fourth Point, If Present					
G-5. Length of Fifth Point, If Present					
G-6. Length of Sixth Point, If Present					
G-7. Length of Seventh Point, If Present					
H-1. Circumference at Smallest Place Between Burr and First Point					
H-2. Circumference at Smallest Place Between First and Second Points					
H-3. Circumference at Smallest Place Between Second and Third Points					
H-4. Circumference at Smallest Place Between Third and Fourth Points or half way between Third Point and Beam Tip if Fourth Point is missing.					
TOTALS					

ADD	Column 1		Location of Kill:	(County)	(State/Prov)
	Column 2		Date Killed:	Hunter:	
	Column 3		Owner:	Telephone #: ( )	
	Subtotal		Owner's Address:		
	SUBTRACT Column 4		Guide's Name and Address:		
	FINAL SCORE		Remarks: (Mention Any Abnormalities or Unique Qualities)		

Here are is a score sheet for whitetail and coues deer. The instructions are on the following page.

I, _____ , certify that I have measured this trophy on _____
PRINT NAME   MM/DD/YYYYY

at _____
STREET ADDRESS   CITY   STATE/PROVINCE   ZIP CODE

and that these measurements and data are, to the best of my knowledge and belief, made in accordance with the instructions given.

Witness: _____ Signature: _____
TO MEASURER'S SIGNATURE   P&Y OFFICIAL MEASURER

_____
ADDRESS

_____
CITY   STATE/PROVINCE   ZIP

BRIEF INSTRUCTIONS FOR MEASURING TYPICAL WHITETAIL AND COUES' DEER

Measurements must be made with a flexible steel tape or steel cable and recorded to the nearest one-eighth of an inch. To simplify addition, please enter fractional figures in eighths and in proper fractions. Refer to **P & Y Measurer's Manual** for a detailed description of measuring procedures.

A. Number of Points on each antler. To be counted a point, a projection must be at least one inch long AND, at some location at least one inch from the tip, the length of the projection must exceed its width. Beam tip is counted as a point but not measured as a point.

B. Tip to Tip Spread is measured between tips of main beams.

C. Greatest Spread is measured between perpendiculars at a right angle to the center line of the skull at widest part whether across main beams or points.

D. Inside Spread of Main Beam is measured at a right angle to the center line of the skull at widest point between main beams. Enter this measurement again in "Spread Credit" column if it is less than or equal to the length of longer main beam. If greater, enter longer main beam length for Spread Credit.

E. Total of Length of Abnormal Points. Abnormal points are generally considered to be those non-typical in location (such as points originating from a point or from bottom or sides of main beam). Sketch all abnormal points on antler illustration (front of form) showing location and length. Measure in usual manner and enter in appropriate blanks.

F. Length of Main Beam is measured from the center of the lowest outside edge of burr over outer curve to the most distant point of the main beam. Begin measuring at the location on the burr where the center line along the outer curve of the beam intersects the burr.

G-1-2-3-4-5-6-7. Length of Normal Points. Normal points project from the top of the main beam as shown in illustration. They are measured from the top edge of the main beam (baseline), over their outer curve, to their tip. To establish the appropriate baseline, lay a tape or (preferably) a cable on the top edge of the beam on each side of the point and draw a line under the cable to reflect the top edge of the beam as if the point was not present. Record point lengths in appropriate blanks.

H-1-2-3-4. Circumferences. Circumferences are taken at the smallest place between corresponding normal points, as illustrated. If first point is missing, take H-1 and H-2 at smallest place between burr and second point. If G-4 is missing, take H-4 halfway between the center of G-3 and tip of main beam. Circumference measurements must be taken with a steel tape (a cable cannot be used for these measurements).

ENTRY REQUIREMENTS

1. **Original scoring form** completed by an Official Measurer of the Pope & Young Club or the Boone & Crockett Club.
2. **Completed Fair Chase Affidavit.**
3. **Three photos of antlers, horns, or skull** (a view from the front side, a view from the left side and a view from the right side). A field photo is also requested, if possible.
4. **$25.00 recording fee** (made payable to the Pope and Young Club)

Drying Period: To be eligible for entry in the Pope & Young Records, a trophy must first have been stored under normal room temperature and humidity for at least 60 days after date of kill. No trophy will be considered which has been altered in any way from its natural state.

POPE & YOUNG CLUB

Official Scoring System for Bowhunting North American Big Game

MINIMUM SCORE 13 - 8/16	COUGAR	SEX
		☐ Male
		☐ Female

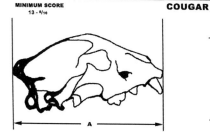 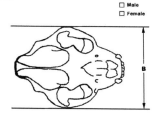

SEE OTHER SIDE FOR INSTRUCTIONS		MEASUREMENTS
A. Greatest Length Without Lower Jaw	(Measured in Sixteenths)	
B. Greatest Width	(Measured in Sixteenths)	
	FINAL SCORE	

Location of Kill: _____ (County) _____ (State/Prov)

Date Killed: _____ Hunter: _____

Owner: _____ Telephone #: ( )

Owner's Address: _____

Guide's Name and Address: _____

Remarks: (Mention Any Abnormalities or Unique Qualities)

Were dogs used in conjunction with the pursuit and harvest of this animal? ☐ YES ☐ NO

If yes, the following statements apply:
1. I was present at the time that the dogs were initially released to pursue this animal.
2. If electronic collars were attached to any of the dogs, at no time from the beginning of the chase until the harvest of this animal were receivers used in the pursuit and harvest.

To the best of my knowledge the above statements are true. If #1 & #2 do not apply, please explain on a seperate sheet.

_____ _____
HUNTER'S SIGNATURE   MM/DD/YYYYY

I, _____ , certify that I have measured this trophy on _____
PRINT NAME   MM/DD/YYYYY

at _____
STREET ADDRESS   CITY   STATE/PROVINCE   ZIP CODE

and that these measurements and data are, to the best of my knowledge and belief, made in accordance with the instructions given.

Witness: _____ Signature: _____
TO MEASURER'S SIGNATURE   P&Y OFFICIAL MEASURER

_____
ADDRESS

_____
CITY   STATE/PROVINCE   ZIP

Here are is a score sheet for cougar/mountain lion. The instructions are on the following page.

BRIEF INSTRUCTIONS FOR MEASURING COUGAR

Measurements must be made with a flexible steel tape and recorded to the nearest one-sixteenth of an inch. Calipers or a skull box may be used. To simplify addition, please enter fractional figures in sixteenths and in proper fractions. Refer to **P & Y Measurer's Manual** for a detailed description of measuring procedures.

A. **Greatest Length** is measured between perpendiculars to the long axis of the skull WITHOUT the lower jaw, and EXCLUDING malformations. (Normal teeth are included)

B. **Greatest Width** is measured between perpendiculars at right angles to the long axis.

All adhering flesh, membrane, and cartilage MUST be completely removed before the drying period begins and official measurements are taken.

IF DOGS ARE USED, THE HUNTER MUST BE PRESENT AT THE TIME THE DOGS ARE RELEASED AND NO ELECTRONIC COLLARS CAN BE USED IN THE PURSUIT

ENTRY REQUIREMENTS

1. **Original scoring form** completed by an Official Measurer of the Pope & Young Club or the Boone & Crockett Club.
2. **Completed Fair Chase Affidavit.**
3. **Three photos of antlers, horns, or skull** (a view from the front side, a view from the left side and a view from the right side). A field photo is also requested, if possible. The front view is best taken from above at a 45-degree angle.
4. **$25.00 recording fee** (made payable to the Pope and Young Club)

Drying Period: To be eligible for entry in the Pope & Young Records, a trophy must first have been stored under normal room temperature and humidity for at least 60 days after date of kill. No trophy will be considered which has been altered in any way from its natural state.

All flesh and membrane MUST be removed from skull prior to the drying period.

Appendix B

Game Anatomy for:

Elk
Deer
Black Bear

The following circulatory, skeletal, and digestive system game illustrations are provided by the National Bowhunter Education Foundation (NBEF). Permission has been granted from the NBEF for use of these copyrighted materials in this book.

ELK

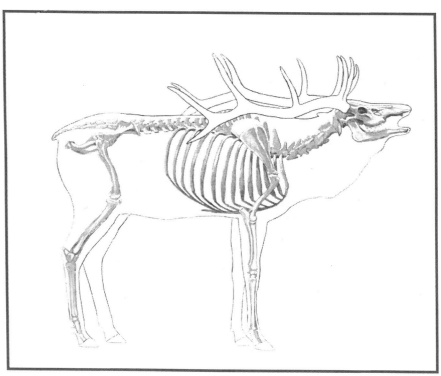

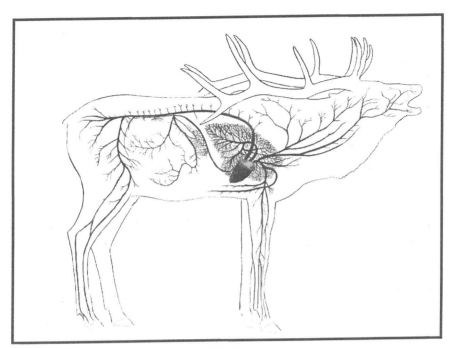

ELK

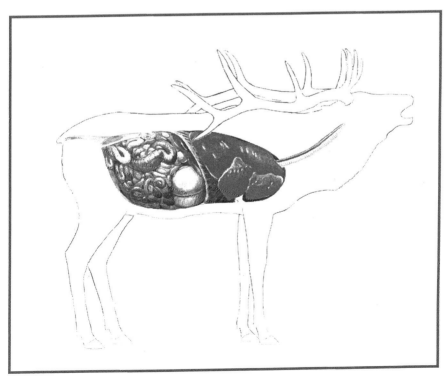

© 2005 National Bowhunter Education Foundation

WHITE-TAILED DEER

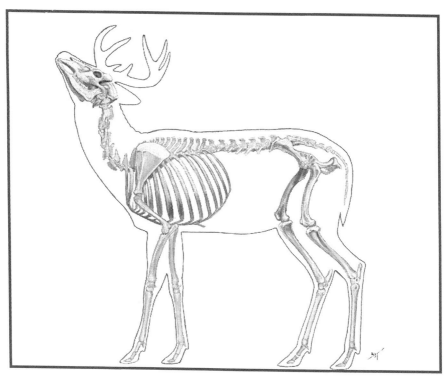

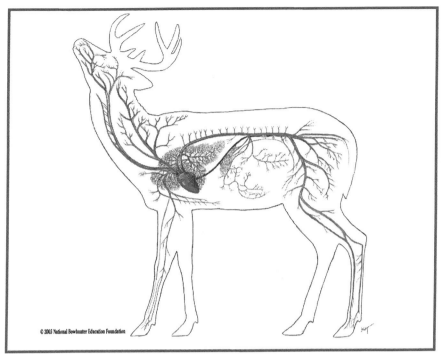

© 2005 National Bowhunter Education Foundation

WHITE-TAILED DEER

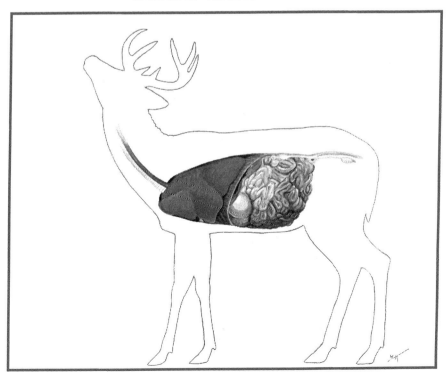

BLACK BEAR

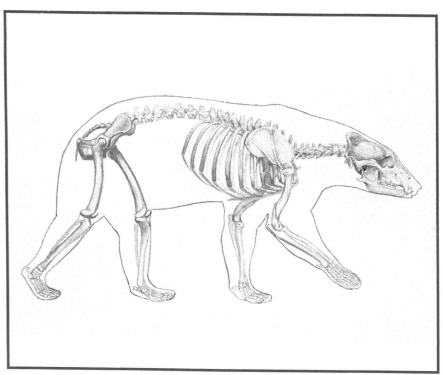

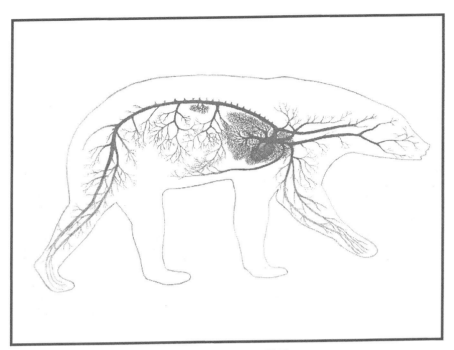

BLACK BEAR

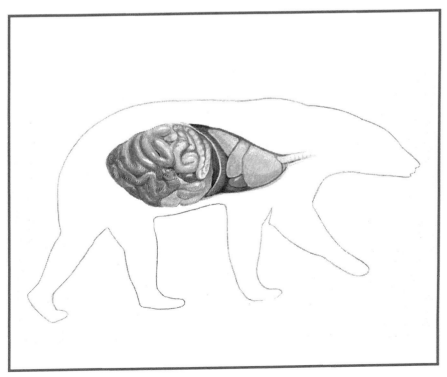

SAVE OUR HERITAGE

"Your Investment in the Future of Archery and Bowhunting"

SAVE OUR HERITAGE

The Save Our Heritage initiative comes from the Archery Trade Association and the Bowhunting Preservation Alliance. With the purchase of this book you are supporting programs that help grow the sports you love-—archery and bowhunting. SOH book proceeds support community archery programs and parks; archery range building and refurbishing; in-school and after-school archery and bowhunting programs; and many more nationwide efforts to grow archery and protect and promote bowhunting.

DID YOU KNOW?

■ ATA has given grants totaling nearly $600,000 to help fund school-archery programs in nearly 40 states.

■ ATA is working to develop Community Archery Programs (CAPs) in urban/suburban areas in Alabama, Arizona, California, Illinois, Iowa, Michigan, Minnesota, Ohio, Tennessee and Nevada.

■ ATA partners with state wildlife agencies to fund archery or shooting program coordinators who lead CAP efforts on a local level.

■ ATA paid for a research study that analyzed the effectiveness of school archery programs and created the Insight brochure summarizing the results. The brochure helps administrators and others understand the value of school archery programs.

■ ATA created the Insight brochure, Archery, the Safe Sport, which is an invaluable tool when discussing the safety aspects of archery with school and recreation program administrators.

■ ATA education staff members created Explore Bowhunting, an intro-ductory bowhunting curriculum available to educators and program managers.

■ ATA works with state agencies to locate archery parks in areas where kids, families and other community citizens recreate.

■ ATA works with state agencies to develop urban deer hunting oppor-tunities.

■ ATA partnered with the U.S. Fish and Wildlife Service to offer more bowhunting opportunities on National Wildlife Refuges.

■ ATA has provided legal defense for private landowners whose right to bowhunt has been challenged by neighbors, local groups or even residential associations.

Your support of the Save Our Heritage program provides funds for these programs . . . and more.

LOOKING FOR AN ARCHERY RETAILER?

ARCHERYSEARCH ◎ COM

LOOKING FOR AN ARCHERY INSTRUCTOR?

ARCHERYSEARCH ◎ COM

LOOKING FOR AN ARCHERY RANGE?

ARCHERYSEARCH ◎ COM

LOOKING FOR AN ARCHERY CLUB?

ARCHERYSEARCH ◎ COM

Where you'll find all the
answers to your archery and
bowhunting questions

Other titles available from the Save Our Heritage book program include:

208 pages, 140+ photos, color insert, Hardcover $24.95	208 pages, 80+ photos, color insert, Hardcover $24.95	208 pages, 100+ photos, color insert, Hardcover $24.95	240 pages, 80+ photos, color insert, Hardcover $24.95

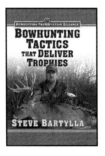

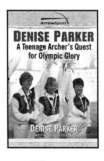

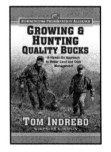

240 pages, 100+ photos, Hardcover $24.95	208 pages, 80+ photos, color insert, Hardcover $24.95	176 pages, 70+ photos, Paperback $19.95	176 pages, 100+ photos, & DVD Paperback $24.95

Ask for these exciting and informative titles at your local sporting goods dealer or order on-line at www.atabooks.com. Call our office at 1-800-652-7527 or write to us at Woods N' Water Press, P.O. Box 550, Florida, NY 10921 for a catalog. We thank you for your support!

SAVE OUR HERITAGE

These are the ONLY books you can buy where a portion of every sale goes back to save your bowhunting heritage!